# NOW FAITH!

## PRACTICING FAITH IN THE LORD NOW

*"Now faith is the substance of things hoped for, the evidence of things not seen....Without faith it is impossible to please Him, for the one who comes to God must believe that He is, and that He is a rewarder of those who diligently seek Him"* (Hebrews 11:1,6, NKJV).

## DAN BOHI

BECOMING LOVE MEDIA GROUP

Copyright © 2023 Dan Bohi

*Now Faith! Practicing Faith in the Lord Now / Dan Bohi*

Published by Becoming Love Media Group

ISBN: 978-1-7361421-4-1

All rights reserved. No portion of this publication may be reproduced, stored in a retrieval system, or transmitted in any form or by any means, except for brief quotations in printed reviews, without prior permission of Rev. Jim Williams. Requests may be submitted by email: **jimwilliams@becomingloveministries.com**

All Scripture quotations, unless otherwise indicated, are taken from the New American Standard Bible, © 1960, 1962, 1963, 1968, 1971, 1972, 1973, 1975, 1977, 1995 by The Lockman Foundation. Used by permission.

Cover and interior design by D.E. West - www.zaqdesigns.com
 with Dust Jacket Press Creative Services

Faith icons created by Freepik - Flaticon.com
Cover photos purchased from Adobe Stock

Printed in the United States

BECOMING LOVE MEDIA GROUP

# CONTENTS

FOREWORD ............................................................. v
ACKNOWLEDGMENTS ............................................. ix
INTRODUCTION ..................................................... xi

1 FAITHING IN JESUS NOW AND FOREVER ................. 1
2 LIVING BY FAITH IN THE WORD OF GOD ................ 25
3 BELIEVING WHAT GOD HAS ALREADY DONE ........ 47
4 REIGNING IN OUR HEARTS ALREADY ................... 67
5 LIVING BY FAITH, NOT BY FLESH ......................... 87
6 PRACTICING DAILY RELATIONSHIP
   IN THE LORD BY FAITH ........................................ 107
7 GROWING FROM FAITH TO FAITH
   THAT ACTS AND WORKS ...................................... 127
8 ACTIVATING FAITH GROWS MORE FAITH ............ 145
9 CORRESPONDING ACTIONS WITH OUR FAITH ..... 159
10 OVERFLOWING WITH HOPE ................................ 177
11 BELIEVING AND CONFESSING GOD'S
    WORD WORK TOGETHER ..................................... 195
12 DECLARING BY FAITH THE WORD
    OF GOD OVER OURSELVES .................................. 213

ABOUT DAN BOHI ..................................................... 235

# FOREWORD

*"Now faith is the certainty of things hoped for,
and the evidence of things not seen"*
(Hebrews 11:1)

Dan Bohi was raised with bold Kingdom heritage and family impact. In 1995, he endured an auto calamity that traumatized him near fatality but transformed his eternity. This tragedy wrecked his body, robbed varsity athletic agility, destroyed his construction industry, and depleted currency from him, his wife Debbie, and their family.

By faith, the Lord removed futility, restored mobility, forgave iniquity, and cleansed impurity. The Lord now increases in Dan humility, grows maturity, and renews fidelity to Jesus and intimacy in the Spirit. Late in 2008, God called him into ministry with one priority: becoming love in Jesus!

The Holy Spirit called and qualified Dan Bohi to proclaim faith based on the Word of God. Now, Dan and Debbie lead Becoming Love Ministries Association, teamed with nine colleagues and couples with accountability to a dynamic non-profit board. Within this team of Spirit-anointed servant leaders, my wife Carol and I are blessed to serve with Dan and his team among congregations, denominations, generations, and nations.

In 2010, we first heard Dan preach at a church near Kansas City. When he spoke the next year during a national evangelism conference plenary session, hundreds of pastors and leaders responded for prayer. Beginning in 2012, Dan participated in national prayer summits we hosted at the Global Ministry Center (GMC) and at church facilities in Kansas City. To the praise of God's glory, during these 15 years, Dan has preached in more than 1,500 churches.

In 2014, Carol and I first conversed deeply with Dan and Debbie during dinner in our Kansas City home. Soon, the Lord revealed to Dan in a dream that I would resign at the GMC, and we would move to Jerusalem. The Holy Spirit challenged Dan to invite us to partner with him while he helped to support our ministries there. After four years ministering in Israel, the Lord led us back to the USA to help care for elderly parents and to advance *Becoming Love Ministries*. Now, this entire team is pursuing together the call of the Holy Spirit who fulfills each of us in Yeshua Messiah through global ministries, including several based in Jerusalem.

The Lord began to enable Dan and the *Becoming Love Ministries* team to invest in other mission leaders, apostles, prophets, evangelists, pastors, teachers, ministry organizations, and international revival movements. All of these team ministries thrive through partners who give sacrificially, generously, and monthly. The vision for global impact through Becoming Love in Jesus is achieving reality daily through persons and partners such as you and your family.

Several *Becoming Love Ministries* colleagues helped to edit *Now Faith* by Dan. Each section grips and compels all of us to stretch authentic faith in Jesus. Throughout these 12 chapters, Dan proclaims and practices faith in the Lord and the Word of God in holiness and purity of heart and life. As a result, more leaders and congregations experience deep cleansing from God in tandem with the supernatural power of the Spirit demonstrated in extraordinary miracles.

Dan's preaching and writing is fervent in fusion of the Word and Spirit to empower leaders and congregations globally. He preaches a lifestyle of intimacy with Christ in which each of us activates the Word, reproducing a lifestyle of worship naturally in the supernatural.

I commend wholeheartedly Dan's priority for the Word of God and insights on faith. As we read this book with a prayerful mind and healthy courage, the LORD will change our lives and add our names to a list of His mighty ones: faithful servants of King Yeshua, valiant victors, fearless overcomers, experienced in exploits, and cherished champions.

We pray for you who receive and believe *Now Faith*. With you, by faith in Jesus, we are becoming love.

Daniel D. Ketchum, Ph.D.
*Becoming Love Ministries*

# ACKNOWLEDGMENTS

I am deeply grateful for the tenacious work of my editor Dr. Daniel Ketchum. Your work on this book is truly a gift from God. Your keen eye to detail is second to none. Thank you for your many hours of hard work that will impact the Kingdom of God in ways only eternity will reveal. You are truly a grammar hammer!

I am deeply grateful to the Rev. Jim Williams for producing and investing in this book. It has not gone unnoticed, and I am extremely grateful for your partnership as Executive Director of Becoming Love Ministries.

I would be remiss if I did not thank the Becoming Love Ministry Board who gives me unwavering support as we fulfill the call to wake up the church to the power, purity and freedom of the Spirit-filled life. Without your constant encouragement this would be a difficult task.

Finally, to our partners worldwide that sacrificially give so that we can fulfill our mission. You are a constant encouragement and support as we keep advancing the footprint of the Kingdom. Each one of you are a good and perfect gift from Abba!

# INTRODUCTION

What is Faith? If you were to look up the definition of faith in the dictionary you would find this: Faith is a "complete trust or confidence in someone or something." Hebrews 11:1 says: "Now faith is the substance of things hoped for, the evidence of things not seen." (NKJV) Let's talk about active faith or as the book suggest, *Now Faith*. Dan Bohi gives insight into what *Now Faith* consists of when he suggests that "Faith is a *power* and a *substance* that is innate and a part of the actual DNA of God." In other words, faith is rooted in the Word of God.

As you read this book you will become convinced that Dan Bohi sees faith not merely as something that we practice like we participate in an activity or hobby, no, faith is much more than mere practice. Faith is power, faith is a force to be reckoned with. When we have *Now Faith*, we begin to release into our lives unlimited possibilities in the spiritual realm. When Dan Bohi suggests that faith is a power and a substance, he means that when you have faith you are connecting into a power source that is part of the DNA or the heart of God. We are connecting to that same power through His word that spoke worlds into existence. You can't separate God from His word!

One of the great thoughts in this book is the fact that salvation is more than just a get out of hell and entrance into heaven reality. No, Dan suggests that salvation describes the total victory and prosperity that Jesus provides for your total man. *Now Faith* allows us to understand that Christ has provided everything we need for life and Godliness.

Righteousness is the work that is done by the Spirit of the Living God in a moment in time. Simply understood, it is when we were put in right standing with God and because we are in right relationship with God we then can be in right relationship with others around us. This only happens by the power of the Holy Spirit that lives inside of us. Jesus reminded us that it better that the Spirit live inside you, than walk beside you. As Dan states: "Faith is the power and substance that releases the righteousness of God from our spirit, into our bodies and into our souls and into the circumstances around us."

We understand two words as they relate to faith. The first is substance and the second is power. Let's look at the word substance. We sometimes understand substance as the principal or necessary part of something. Faith is a substance or a principal or necessary ingredient of what we are hoping for. And if faith is power and our faith is grounded in a power source then that would mean that our *Now Faith* is grounded in the Word of God. It is God's word that is the generator that produces our desires in which we hope for. The second word is power which is always found in the Word of God. The power of our faith is found in the written or spoken word of God. Think about the power of His spoken word! Think about creation, amazing, nothing was created unless God spoke it into existence. Now that's power.

The power of our *Faith* is in His word. That is why we should not neglect such an incredible gift. It is the Word of God that activates our faith in our present circumstances so that we live not by what we see with our physical eyes but by what we know is true based on God's word. You won't journey very far in this book without agreeing that we can base our words, our lives and our actions by faith in the Word of God. This is the fight of faith. When we engage in this fight we will release the substance, the power that is only found in His Word. Come on, take this journey into faith that is constant and present in every moment of our lives.

Rev. Jim Williams
*Executive Director Becoming Love Ministries*
*Bethany, Oklahoma*

# 1
# FAITHING IN JESUS NOW AND FOREVER!

"I am not ashamed of the gospel, because it is the power of God for the salvation of everyone who believes" (Romans 1:16). When Jesus transformed Paul's life, he wrote these words.

I believe Jesus transformed my life by faith in Him, a miracle I will recount in this book. Now, I believe. I believe Jesus. I believe His miracle power for salvation of all who believe. Do you believe? Do you experience "Now Faith"?

In Hebrews 11: 1 we read, "Now faith is the certainty of things hoped for, and the evidence of things not seen. Now faith is the certainty or substance of things hoped for, and the proof or evidence of things not seen."

In this book and in our world now for such a time as this, I relate stories of people who received and practiced "Now Faith" and overcame fear. My father-in-law, Dr. Don Owens, the father of my wife Debbie, tells two of these stories. Here is his first account of now faith.

When my father-in-law went to New Guinea to ordain new pastors, he saw five guys carrying a man who had no hands and no feet. He had legs and arms, but he had no hands and no feet. Also, half of that man's tongue was cut off.

My father-in-law asked the man being carried, "What happened?" The man uttered, "Oh, I went to a village, and I preached the gospel. Several men said that if I didn't stop preaching about Jesus, they were going to cut my hand off. And I said, 'Well, I cannot and will not stop.'" So, they cut his hand off.

About a month and a half later, when his hand healed a little, he went back and preached again. And they said, "If you don't shut up, we're going to cut off your other hand." So, he lost his other hand. When he healed, he went back again, and they told him they would cut off his foot. He kept proclaiming Jesus, so they cut his foot off.

After he healed, he went back to preach again, and the men threatened to take his other foot. He taught the love of Jesus again and they kept their word to cut off his other foot. He went back and they said, "We're going to cut your tongue out, so you can't talk about Jesus." Well, they only got half of his tongue, so he could still talk.

So, my father-in-law asked the man being carried, "What happened to those guys who nearly killed you?" The man said, "Well, the five guys you are ordaining tonight are the men who did this to me. These men saw they could not defeat the love and power of Jesus in me, because I had faith that established me in the midst of persecution. They wanted to know my Jesus. Now they are all pastoring churches and the Gospel is expanding, even exploding."

Again, "The Gospel is the power of God for the salvation of everyone who believes!" And again, I ask, "Do we believe now? Do we have now faith?

In Luke 18:8, Jesus asks, "When the Son of Man returns, will He find faith on the earth?" That question has inspired and motivated me to dig out realities of faith. As we study many Bible passages, we will learn more together about possibilities of faith: believing now.

## NOW FAITH!

I have been drafting a definition of faith; here is my latest attempt. **Faith is a power and a substance that is innate and a part of the actual DNA of God's Word.** The Word of God is part of God Himself. The Word of God is the LORD Himself speaking and revealing Himself and truth to us.

So, faith is a power: the power of substance. Faith is a part of the DNA of God's Word. We cannot separate God from His Word. Faith is not something we merely practice or exercise. Faith is a power. It is a force. I believe there are unending possibilities in the realm of faith.

When we are teaching on themes such as faith, we should avoid causing people to feel we are prideful or arrogant. We cannot simply tell God to do things and expect He will do them. So, we must always teach with love and humility. I repeat. We will always teach with love and humility.

In other words, we should never take some truth and say, "This is THE Truth." We should never receive some new revelation ourselves and begin to say, "This is the truth now." Why? Because that is how cults start. That is how churches divide. Instead, we should say, "Let's study and practice truth that points to and clarifies THE Truth." THE truth is the Person Jesus Christ and His power that sets us free.

Let's start in Romans chapter one, verse 11: "I long to see you so that I may impart some spiritual gift to you, so that you might be established, to make you strong."

So, Paul was eager to get to Rome to impart a supernatural charisma to the believers, so they could be established...established in the middle of persecution. Do you hear that? I want you to know persecution is coming. Do we sense that and are we ready?

I opened this chapter by sharing an amazing story of faith without fear. I relay another story now from my father-in-law, Dr. Don Owens, the father of my wife, Debbie. Both of these are stories of people who were established and could not be moved.

Dr. Owens was in Nashville at a conference where a Vietnamese man was speaking. This man had been a prisoner of war in a Vietnamese prisoner of war camp led by Communists. He told stories about days he and all prisoners were desperately hungry.

Finally, he believed he was led by the Lord to stand alone by a fence right next to a river. Soon, fish would jump out of the river, and he could grab them, cook them, and eat them. Nobody knew how he got his food. But he knew the story in 1 Kings 17 of ravens feeding Elijah, which was like miracles of God keeping this Christian Vietnamese man alive in a prisoner of war camp when everybody else was starving.

Men who controlled those prisoners tortured him to try to force him to give up his faith, but he never did. Then one day, the Colonel in charge of the prisoner of war camp said, "If you don't renounce Jesus, I'm going to shoot you in the head tomorrow morning at seven o'clock near the flagpole."

That night after he was threatened to death, the Colonel got drunk, was hung over the next morning, and slept in until he was mostly sober. Then, he looked into that foggy jungle morning and saw that little Christian man standing out there by the flagpole, waiting to be shot. With faith in God, he was ready and waiting for the Colonel.

So, the officer splashed cold water, got dressed, and walked arrogantly to the flagpole. He cocked the gun in his hand, and said, "This is your last chance." The little Christian man said, "I will not denounce this Jesus! He is my life!"

The Colonel pointed, pulled the trigger, and the gun would not fire. So, he glanced at a guard, pointed the gun up, pulled the trigger, and the gun shot into the air. So, he cocked the gun again, pressed it against the Christian's head, and shouted, "I am not joking! This is your last chance."

The Vietnamese believer responded slowly and confidently, "You can shoot me. I have already given my life to Jesus. I will not renounce my Savior."

The officer pulled the trigger again. It did not fire. He cussed and when he threw the gun on the ground, it fired. Everyone jumped, except the stunned Colonel who stood still and silent.

So, my father-in-law was talking to this same Vietnamese Christian speaker at a Nashville conference. Dr. Owens asked him, "What happened to that officer?" The speaker pointed to a taller, stronger man nearby and said, "Oh, that's him." The Colonel was the guy now carrying the believer's bags.

Wherever this faith-filled Vietnamese preacher traveled around the world, declaring faith in God, the once-opposing officer who tried to kill him with a gun that wouldn't work, was now carrying his luggage all over the world. He was now serving Christ, because he had been established through a humble witness and a supernatural impartation of the Holy Spirit.

Those are examples of Christians similar to believers we might know who are solid in faith and will not be moved. The power of the gospel cannot be stopped, if it's the true gospel.

Now, let's return to Romans 1:15-16: "That is why I am so eager to preach the gospel also to you who are in Rome. For I am not ashamed of the gospel." Friend, isn't that a strong statement? "I am not ashamed of the gospel, because it is the power of God that brings salvation to everyone who believes." The gospel is the power of God for salvation!

Do you know that "salvation" is a word that describes the total victory and prosperity the LORD provides for your spirit, your soul, and your body? Do we agree that "salvation" is the meaning of the name Jesus? This gospel of Jesus Christ is the total divine prosperity package, providing whatever our spirit needs, our soul needs, and our body needs. That is salvation.

Paul declares to the community of faith persecuted in Rome, "I am not ashamed of salvation. I am not ashamed of the gospel." Why? Because in the gospel, the power of God produces salvation. This is one major reason we are studying these Scriptures together!

Is this power available to everyone who performs? No, the Word does not say that. To everyone who works harder? No, the Word does not say that either. What is this power? Where is this power? Who is eligible for this power? The Bible says, "To everyone who believes." Remember, we are learning about real faith. But isn't this power of salvation for everyone who keeps the rules? No. I am not teaching on law. I'm teaching on faith!

This gospel is the power of God. This gospel brings salvation (Jesus) "to everyone who believes: first to the Jew, then to the Gentile."

Verse 17: "For in the gospel the righteousness...." Listen to this: "The righteousness of God is revealed."

How? From faith...to faith...to faith...to faith...and more faith...from first to last. "Just as it is written, 'The righteous one will live by faith.'" Not by striving, not by worrying, not by stressing. But by faith!

What is righteousness? Righteousness is what the Holy Spirit accomplishes in our spirit in a moment in time. Righteousness is right relationship with God that results in right relationship with others.

# NOW FAITH!

Faith is the path that releases the righteousness of God from our spirit, into our bodies, into our souls, and into the circumstances of life around us. That is why I think we will learn more about faith for the rest of our days until Yeshua returns. Amen?

Now, I emphasize again that we should always teach with love and humility. Proverbs 16:21 is a verse the Lord has given me like new. Look with me at this: "The wise in heart will be called understanding, and sweet speech increases persuasiveness." In other words, we can teach the hardest truth if our speech is sweet with love and humility.

People will not put up their walls in defense, shut us off, or turn us off, if our speech is sweet, kind, caring. If our faith is motivated with love, we can persuade. Paul wrote in Galatians 5:6, "The only thing that matters is faith working through love." If we are trying to speak truth without being motivated by love, all it does is give people knowledge, which merely puffs up.

But if we are trying to speak the truth in love, as Paul taught in Ephesians 4:15, then God's edifying grace establishes people for what is coming in these end times. So, if the speech of our lips is motivated by love, the unchangeable message of truth will be accepted by more and more people. Right?

Let's return now to Hebrews 11 and consider this theme on faith as a powerful substance. In Hebrews 11:1 we read, "Now faith is the certainty of things hoped for, and the evidence of things not seen." Read this aloud with me: now faith is the certainty or substance of things hoped for, and the proof or evidence of things not seen.

Now faith is the substance--the certainty--the substance of what we're hoping for. So, faith is a substance that is power found in God's Word to provide our desires, because what we hope flows from our desires.

Let's look closer at two words that describe faith in a different angle. Note the two words on either side of the word "faith". The Bible says, "Now faith is..."

"Now": present tense. "Is": present tense. "Now, faith is."

Now faith is practicing faith in the Lord now.

Let me give you another angle on Faith. Together in the Spirit of the Lord, we will gain and even seize a lot of new discoveries about faith in the following chapters.

How do we know Jesus is the faithful one? I want each of us to get this. Faith is the substance of what we desire, of what we are hoping for. So, ultimately, what is the substance of faith? Jesus! Jesus is the desire of all nations. Do we understand this yet? The true essence or substance of faith is Jesus. Not something. Someone: The One!

In Hebrews 13:8 we read, "Jesus is the same yesterday, today, and forever." So, what is faith and what does faith do? How do we appropriate or receive faith? How do we walk in faith? How do we live by faith? Faith is the power that brings the Jesus of yesterday and the Jesus of forever into right now. History into eternity. Faithing in Jesus is now and forever!

We know what Jesus did yesterday, because we can read about it in the Bible. And we know what He is going to do in the future, because we can read about it in the Bible. But faith brings us to right now. Now, faith is. Is!

So, the only way we can operate in faith is to receive it from the Word of God, the Bible. We cannot operate in faith by someone else's opinion or by someone else's words. We can only get to God's reality by getting into the Word of God ourselves. Because the Word of God

# NOW FAITH!

is where faith exists. The DNA of faith is found in the actual Word of God.

Now faith comes by hearing and hearing by the word of Christ. Now faith is made perfect by seeing Jesus, the Word made flesh. Again, the essence or substance of faith is in the God-Man and the Word: Christ Jesus and His Word, the whole Bible.

While we explore and apply faith, we will search verses that encourage us to get more involved in what the Word says instead of what others say with other words. For example, let's embrace 2 Corinthians chapter one, verse 20 where Paul writes, "The promises of God are many. In Jesus they are Yes. Therefore, through Him also is our 'Amen' to the glory of God through us." God is waiting on our faith and agreement to what He has already said "Yes" to. The promises do not become "Yes" to us until our faith agreement enables them to be our reality.

In God's Word, He has given believers more than 8,000 promises. Remember the verse we noted? "I am not ashamed of the gospel, because it is the power of God unto salvation for those who believe." So, every believer has access to over 8,000 promises that are already stamped "Approved" with Jesus' "Yes!" on each promise. He is waiting to give us this faith. And He is waiting for us to receive it and agree.

If we do not get into the Word, if we do not receive what actually is ours, then we will never want to "Amen" what God says about us. If we don't get into the Word, our lives are an "Amen" to what the devil says about us. But now faith comes by hearing, and hearing by the words of Christ. He is releasing the substance of the desires we have in real time: now!

So, faith is the substance of what we desire. Then, fear is the substance of what we don't want. Fear is the substance of what we don't desire.

Fear and faith are opposites. Faith comes by hearing the words of Christ. Fear comes by hearing other words. We have a choice, a free will to choose. We can receive the Messiah's power to say about ourselves what God says about us, instead of what the devil says about us.

The devil says we'll never be healed. The devil says we'll never get ahead. The devil says our family will never be saved. The devil says our church will never experience revival or transform our city. The devil says some persons will never break through.

God's Word says the exact opposite. Faith comes by hearing the words of God. Fear comes by hearing the words of the world. All the promises of God are already "Yes."

Let's remember Jesus' teaching, "I gave you the keys to the kingdom. Whatever you bind on earth has already been bound in heaven. And whatever you loose on earth, has already been loosed in heaven." What was He saying? "I have already said 'Yes'. Now, I am waiting for someone to believe. I have already done the work. I have already provided. I have already sacrificed My blood for your salvation. Now, I am waiting on you to believe the possibilities that are endless if you totally believe!"

Amen. Are we receiving and believing this? Now?

Let's look at Romans 3:21, "Now apart from the law, the righteousness of God has been revealed, being witnessed by the Law and the Prophets. But it is the righteousness of God through faith in Jesus Christ, for all those who believe, since there is no distinction between Jew and Gentile. For all have sinned and fall short of the glory of God, being justified as a gift by His grace, through the redemption that is in Christ Jesus, whom God displayed publicly as a sacrifice of atonement in his blood to be received by faith."

# NOW FAITH!

God demonstrated faith when He provided the blood of Christ, so we could actually receive faith. God worked with faith to demonstrate His righteousness. In God's merciful restraint, He let the sins previously committed go unpunished. He did this to demonstrate his righteousness now--at the present time--so as to be just and the one who justifies those who have faith in Jesus. Can we see how many times the words "faith" and "righteousness" are evident in this passage?

Now, look at verse 27. Where then is boasting? It has been excluded. By what kind of law? By a law of works? No. We are justified and redeemed by the law or principle that requires faith.

Do we really see this? Brothers and sisters, I propose that as we go on this 12-chapter journey, that the law of faith is a key principle of the New Covenant. Some refer to the Old Covenant as the law of works. Nobody can keep all the laws in the Old Covenant, so working to be redeemed by law does not work. Everybody who believes is fulfilling the principle of faith. Are you with me? This is a really big deal.

In Romans 3:31 we read: "Do we then nullify the law by this faith? Far from it! On the contrary, we establish or uphold the law. Paul does not recommend or condone going back to the law of Moses. He's talking about us establishing the law of faith, the principle of faith!

We're supposed to be walking in the new principle of faith that works through love, not performance. Amen? Faith is the law of the New Covenant. The Lord offers to plant this truth first in our heart and in our spirit. Then, faith can help transform our minds and our bodies.

I want each of us to realize the dilemma we are in. Paul wrote in Romans 8:5-7, "Those who are in accord with the flesh, set their minds on the things of the flesh. But those who are in accord with the Spirit, set their minds on the things of the Spirit. For the mind set on the flesh is death, but the mind controlled by the Spirit is life and peace. The mind set on the flesh is hostile towards God. For it does not submit to the law of God, for it is not even able to do so."

Paul is not writing about subjecting ourselves to Old Covenant law. He is teaching us to submit ourselves to the new law of faith, trusting in Jesus alone, faithing only into Christ. Do you see this? To live controlled by the flesh means we try to do things by ourselves to earn God's approval. We try to keep 613 laws and commandments. And the flesh-self wants to brag about how many of the 613 laws we keep compared to how many of the 613 others keep. It's always a comparison of what we ourselves can do. If you're set on that mindset, you cannot enter into the new law of faith.

Paul writes in Romans 8:9-10, "You are not in the flesh or controlled by sinful nature, but in the Spirit, if indeed the Spirit of God lives in you. If anyone does not have the Spirit of Christ, that person does not belong to Christ. But if Christ is in you, your body is dead because of sin, yet your spirit is alive because of righteousness." The Messiah and the Spirit in us provide righteousness: right relationships with Jesus and others!

We remember that Christ-likeness is revealed to the world through people who have received the power of the gospel through faith. Faith is in our spirit. The righteousness of God is in our spirit, waiting to for us to live faith. So, it can change our thoughts, our reactions, our words, our body. In fact, look at Romans 8:11, which is amazing: "If the Spirit of Him who raised Jesus from the dead is living in you, He who raised the Messiah from the dead will also give life to your physical bodies through His Spirit who dwells in you."

Remember that in Luke 18:8, Jesus asked, "When the Son of Man comes back, will He find faith on the earth?" The life of faith Jesus modeled and desires for each of us a lifestyle that releases through

## NOW FAITH!

our right spirit supernatural things from the Kingdom of God into our soul and body and through us into people and circumstances around us. That is the life of faith. Come on! The possibilities are endless!

Many of us who have been on weekly video gatherings together know a lady in Illinois who is suffering and confined to her bed. Even if some do not know her, think for a moment about her and possibilities of now faith. The same Spirit that raised Jesus from the dead is alive in her and can flow out of her spirit to resurrect her body. That's a possibility of faith.

Do you understand the possibilities of faith? Jesus declared, "All things are possible to the one who believes." "All things" would cover a person in paralysis on a bed who needs resurrection. That is included in "all things". Do you see why we need to be so adamant, determined, and resolved to receive the principle and practice of faith? It's amazing!

Let's look at this: now faith is the substance of things we are desiring, right? Yes, faith is the substance of things we are hoping for and the evidence of things we cannot yet see physically. But we "see" them by faith now. We have to start where we're at.

I cannot start where John G. Lake, Oral Roberts, or Billy Graham were. I can't start where Randy Clark is. I have to start right where I am. I have to start with the Faithful One who's willing to walk step by step with me right where I am now. So, if we're comparing ourselves to others, we are going back to the law. We need to start living the faith right now, where we're at. Come on! We need to get our eyes off ourselves and others. We need to fix our eyes on the Faithful One: Jesus Christ.

We have to start where we are. We have to learn what doesn't work. And we are only going to learn that by trial and error. I used to do some pretty dumb stuff, thinking it was faith. I prefer not to talk about it, but I learned what doesn't work. I will tell you that this past year has been my favorite year of ministry since I the LORD called me into ministry. Although I have preached in an average of more than eight services a week this entire year, I feel like I haven't worked.

I've seen more miracles this past year than I have ever seen. And I'm not working! Do you know what I'm doing? I am believing. I'm actually believing in the power of the Word. I have not asked God or prayed for one healing. Instead, I am releasing the Word of God into people's bodies. I am declaring the Word of God into people's souls: their will, mind, and emotions.

One night after I preached the Word and during a healing service, people lined up for prayer all the way to the back of the room. The Lord showed me what each person needed. I spoke a few words to each of them, their tears flowed, and they received words of discernment from the Spirit. I will not work hard in the flesh by going back to the law. I will remain in grace and right relationship (righteousness) with Jesus and people in need. I will live the faith "not by might or power, but by the Spirit, says the Lord Almighty."

Romans 10:17 reminds us, "Faith comes by hearing and hearing by the word of Christ." Right? Faith comes when we hear the word of Christ, which is the Bible. So, we need to speak the Word of the Lord more than to speak what anybody else says. Also, regarding faith, James 1:26 teaches that a person who claims to have religion, but has not yet learned to bridle the tongue, that person has deceived himself or herself.

Now if faith comes by hearing the word of Christ, we can by faith perceive the Word and the Spirit speaking in our inner ear, our inner spirit. And from my previous teachings, we realize that the LORD created our spirit to produce the seed we put in it. Right? The LORD created our soul and our spirit with the capability to put whatever it needs to make the seed work.

Sometimes in private settings, we think thoughts or speak words such as "I'm tired, I'm sick, I'm depressed, I don't want to live, or I don't know why I can't get a breakthrough." Those thoughts or words settle in our heart and our heart thinks that what we just thought or said is what we actually want. Then, our heart tries to produce those thoughts or words as our reality.

Other times in public settings, we might say words that sound spiritual or mature or what we want people to hear. Then, our heart hears those conflicting words, and our hearts become confused and deceived. Why? Because sometimes, our heart hears we don't want to live, but other times, our heart hears we want everybody else to live. Some of us have not yet learned to speak words about ourselves and others based only on the Word of God.

If we speak negative feelings about ourselves or others, then critical thought patterns, fears, worries, and concerns accumulate in our soul. Our heart hears all that, and our heart thinks the words we speak are what we intend or desire. However, if we think, speak, and talk about ourselves and others consistently the way God speaks about us faith-fully, our heart could and would produce that faith reality all the time. Amen?

So, the Word and Spirit give us faith to activate what we cannot see. Right? This is very important. Faith is the evidence of things we cannot see. I don't need faith for my desk chair, because I see it and touch it. I don't need faith for my phone that plays my background music, because I can hear it. I don't need faith, for what I can see or hear with my senses. I don't need faith for that. But I need faith for what I cannot see or hear. I cannot walk in faith for what I cannot see, unless that gift of faith is based on the Word of God and what the Lord says.

In 2 Corinthians 4:18, Paul writes, "Therefore, we do not fix our eyes on what is seen, for things that are seen are temporary. Things that are unseen are eternal." So, if we are going to live the life of faith, we refuse to become preoccupied with things we see or thoughts or words that try to draw us out of faith. We all know so much of what we see or hear is designed to talk us out of faith: prices at grocery stores or gas stations, news on TV, our bank account balance, and all kinds of stress. The only way we are going to live consistently authentic, biblical faith is to think in our minds and speak over our lives what God says about us.

That is where faith comes from. Faith from God always sees and always knows. Faith in the Word and Spirit always sees and always knows. When you and I get into the realm of faith, we can know the answer before we see the answer. We can believe the breakthrough before we see the breakthrough. Sometimes we see it by faith. How and why? Because we're not looking at temporary distractions.

One night in Boise, a gentleman took me out for dinner and spent two and a half hours sharing about his life and how God has blessed his life. His name is Mark, a realtor and developer in Boise and the Treasure Valley. He poured into me for two and a half hours until I came away with so much more faith. The last thing he said to me was, "If you ever need anything, call me," and he meant it. This brother is developing Starbucks, Walmarts, Krogers, and subdivisions. I mean, this guy is everywhere. In fact, when I was praying later with a man who had MS Multiple Sclerosis, his son walked in. I asked the boy, "Do you know this man named Mark? He said, "Oh, yeah. I don't know him personally, but his name is on every sign around here."

# NOW FAITH!

Anyway, while Mark was sharing his life in Christ with me for two and a half hours, he proved that faith always sees. Faith always knows. Based on nothing in the natural. Based 100% on what God's Word says! I want to practice this message in faith and not emotion, without getting too fired up in feelings.

Now, let's come to Second Peter together. Look at 2 Peter 1:3, "For His divine power." Who's? God's. "His divine power has granted to us everything pertaining to life and godliness." Do you know what that verse is? That is Peters rendition of Paul's Romans 1:16. Paul says faith is the power of God for salvation. Peter says faith is the power of God for everything that pertains to life and godliness. These are the same description with unique, powerful words of hope!

In this book, we will study twelve teachings on faith, each focused on the same biblical description. We will see how the Lord in the Word applies and practices faith in hundreds of different words and ways. I pray each of us will receive this faith as we study together.

For example, one person living the faith can change their city. As Paul said, God's divine power has granted to us everything (that includes everything) pertaining to life and godliness. Life is our physical life. Godliness is our eternal life. When we believe, when we live by faith and become the righteousness of God in Christ, His power in the gospel provides everything we will ever need for eternity. His power in the gospel is already in our spirit. Everything we will ever need for eternity has been deposited in our spirit, waiting on us to live the faith and to release it into our soul, our body, and our circumstances. That's the gospel. That's the power of Christ in the gospel.

So, whether we are trying to weigh faith, measure it, assess it, or grow it, faith has exactly the same value to produce everything we hope for. Everything in our whole existence in Christ that we desire is the same proper path to faith. And the greater our faith grows, the greater our desires become our reality.

Let me give you a red-letter verse, truth from our Savior highlighted in red ink in some Bibles. Every time I read this verse, I almost drop my microphone. In Matthew 21:22, Jesus declares, "If you believe, you will receive whatever you ask for in prayer."

Does that verse challenge you? Jesus' words in that verse certainly confront and challenge me. Here is the same verse in different words: "Whatever you ask in prayer, believing, you will receive it all." Jesus said that. He speaks the truth; He cannot lie! Pray. Believe. Receive it all.

Jesus challenges us: there is more believing for us to tap into. There is more in His gift of faith and more in our practice of faith than we have even begun to realize. There is more believing than we see at first glance when we merely scratch the surface! Because the power of Jesus and the gospel depend on our faith, He does have more for each of us trying to live by faith.

I wrote this phrase down after that verse. Faith is the evidence. Faith is the only evidence we have until it manifests in our soul and body. We don't have any evidence, except faith!

And we will only receive that manifestation of faith when we base it on what God says about us. So, we must stop listening to what the world, the flesh, and the devil says about us. Amen?

Now, how do we get into this faith life, where the reality of God's Word is the daily life that we're actually living? It's a life walking in the grace of God, right? Yes, now faith is our whole life, walking in the grace of God in every moment of every day!

# NOW FAITH!

In Romans 5:2, we learn that...by faith...we can enter into this grace... by which we stand. Remember, Paul wanted to travel to Rome so he could impart to them spiritual gifts to establish and ground them. He wanted them to experience a grace where they could stand. I propose to you the only way...to live...in the grace of God...is...by... faith...in every now.

In fact, I believe that people who "burn out" have quit living by grace. They "burn out" trying to live by works. I believe it is literally impossible for us to burn out in grace. Why do people hit walls of exhaustion or defeat, get worn down by stress, and run out of steam? I will explain why through a definition of grace the Lord has been burning on my heart. Here it is: Grace is God's willingness to use His power and ability on our behalf, even though we don't deserve it. Again: **Grace is God's willingness to use His power and ability on our behalf, even though we don't deserve it.** The only way we can live in grace is by faith. We enter into grace by faith.

You see why grace is so powerful. God's grace enables us to walk in His power, to live by God's ability. So, when we touch some, they're healed. We touch others, and they're delivered. We touch many, and their lives turn around. We touch a couple, and their marriage is saved. We touch others marginalized, and their family is restored. We touch others for financial blessing, and they receive a thousand-fold return. If we want to live in the ability of God, it's only possible by His grace through faith.

In Hebrews 11:3, we see that everything was created by God's Word. Right? So, in essence, God created everything by using His words. Nothing came into existence without His Word. In John 1:1, a disciple Jesus loved reminds us, "In the beginning was the Word, and the Word was with God, and the Word was God. And all things came into being through Him."

In John 1:1-3, the Lord helps us see three pictures of the Word. The first picture of the Word is the "Logos" or the thoughts of God. The second picture is the spoken Word that came out of God's thoughts. The third picture of the Word is the God-Man Christ Jesus. These three word pictures describe our journey in faith.

Faith starts in our thoughts. As a person thinks within himself or herself, so that person actually is according to Proverbs 23:7. In the beginning are the thoughts of God. Do you know we have the mind of Christ? In our spirit, in the righteousness of God, in Christ who is in our spirit, we have the mind of Christ. We have His thoughts in us. If we let those thoughts produce our words that we will speak, they will manifest in our flesh. Christ became flesh and dwelt among us. The life of faith is believing that everything we will need for eternity... that is already in our spirit is waiting to be released...through our thoughts...that produce our words...that release the grace and power of God...that let us receive all things. That is the life of grace... through...faith.

As Moses wrote in Genesis 1:3, the Spirit of God was hovering over creation and over the waters. It was chaotic, right? The Hebrew word for "waters" can be translated chaos. God's Holy Spirit hovers over chaos. We know and feel a lot of chaotic turbulence in global culture right now.

Now, we meditate on the word "hovering" in the phrase "the Spirit of God was hovering". The Hebrew word for "hovering" means to brood over with anticipation or to crouch down with excitement. So, here's the picture. If we're living in faith, God's Spirit alive in our spirit will be crouched down with expectancy, even in the worst of circumstances!

Do we really understand? Some people fear because it looks like divorce is imminent. Others groan when disease looks terminal. Or

# NOW FAITH!

we panic when it looks like we're going to lose our house. Or we become distressed, because it looks like our ministry is not going to survive.

However, if we are living in the Spirit and in the faith--which means we're in righteousness and right relationship--then, we're in grace. Therefore, instead of circumstances depleting our spiritual zeal, the Holy Spirit living in our spirit quiets stormy, stressful, wild chaos and empowers us to expect, believe, and hope with greater anticipation than we have ever experienced. It's shalom: peace, rest, confidence, wholeness. So, shalom, friends!

How? Why? Because we are preparing to release words that will transform our circumstances. And God said, "Let there be light." God's Spirit is always anticipating breakthrough and revival in the turmoil of the worst situations. He is ready, willing, and able to speak and release His power--His substance--through His words. Now faith is! He is waiting on us to do the same: believe, declare, release!

That is why Paul proclaimed, "I am not ashamed of the gospel, because it is the power of God for the salvation of everyone who believes" (Romans 1:16). Peter affirmed, "The Lord's great power, His divine power has already given us everything that pertains to life and godliness" (2 Peter 1:3).

All of these are practical, precious promises in the Word of God. These reverberate in the Book, waiting on us to agree, declare, and activate them ourselves. Amen? So, God filled His words with spiritual force, the power called faith. This is important, friends! God pronounced His words and filled them with spiritual force, the power called faith.

And we release those words by His Spirit. The rest is history. He enables our words to carry God's power into all of our circumstances.

His Spirit. His power. Our words. In essence, we assert God's faith. We certify God's power by endorsing and repeating His Word to become our word.

After all, we are the Body of Christ. We are the Bride of Christ. And this amazing Good News seems almost too good to be true, doesn't it?

Yet some say, "Brother Dan, you don't understand. I have been saying these things." Well then, keep saying them. Let's keep declaring these truths by faith. If God said it, we are safe in confirming it now!

Let's speak the Word. By the Spirit. With grace. Through faith. If others say something else, something less, something more, or something different, let's stop repeating their opinions.

I will illustrate from my family, all of whom I love. My momma and daddy are past 90. My mom doesn't know how to say anything negative. Everything we talk to mom about is good. "God is on the throne. I can't wait to live longer so I can pray for people more." She releases hope, faith, courage, and excitement. She cannot be defeated: she is living off the fruit of her lips!

By contrast, many things my daddy says are negative. Perhaps the only reason my dad is still around: my momma's atmosphere is greater than his. My dad has seen more positive highs than probably anybody I know. Yet, he still has that subtle undermining. He speaks negative perspectives, which produces his reality.

My dad's glass is usually half empty. My mom's glass is always half full. It's evident in how they talk. Their words are based on what they believe. And what they believe is based on what they think. Do you understand what I mean?

## NOW FAITH!

Do you want to live the faith? I want to live the faith. I will live the faith. Will you live the faith with me? When Jesus comes back, I want all of us to proclaim, "We're faithing! We're declaring! We're decreeing. We're not backing down. Faithing is our reality." Amen?

I'm so thankful, so thankful. I want to pray an impartation that we will live the faith. Can I do that? I long to pray that we will base our words on His Word and will release that substance, that power that is only found in His Word, which is His Person. Will you agree with me?

God, I thank you for these men and women that are hungry for more faith. They're hungry for You. They're hungry for the Word. I pray for a gift of more hunger for each of us. I pray that every one of these men and women will receive the greatest gift, which is more longing and desire for your Word than they have ever experienced. They won't be able to get enough. They will devour Your Word day and night, day and night, day and night. They will not let it depart from their lips. I declare over and into my friends the gift of hunger for Your Word, because that's where the faith is produced.

Then Lord, we trust You to engrave this message on our hearts. So, when stress comes, when delay distracts, when anxiety or chaos pile up, faith will be a deeper mark and reality than temporary feelings that come and go. Let us be people who walk by faith, who live the faith, who please You all the time. Because we live like Jesus. Let us live the key principle of the New Covenant, the practice of faith. I bless my family and my friends with more faith in Jesus' name. Amen.

# 2
# LIVING BY FAITH IN THE WORD OF GOD

In the first chapter, we opened in Romans 1, where Paul proclaimed the power of the gospel for salvation of everyone who will believe. He also taught that God's righteousness is revealed when we live by faith, which comes by hearing, and hearing comes by the Word of Christ.

Also, in chapter one, we studied from Hebrews 11:1, "Now faith is the certainty of things hoped for, and the evidence of things not seen." Now faith is the certainty or substance of things we hope for and desire. Faith is also the proof or evidence of things not yet seen with our eyes.

Let's take a minute to go further and deeper into the substance and power of faith. The substance of faith is the real, actual, tangible, solid presence and power that is innate and latent in the DNA of God's Word. Again, faith is innate in the Word of God. In other words, faith is inherent, intrinsic, and part of the essence of the Word of the LORD.

This faith innate in the Word might be latent or dormant, unrevealed, undiscovered, untapped, or not yet manifested. Nothing would exist if God had not spoken words of faith. I repeat, there would be nothing that is in existence today if the Lord Himself had not spoken words of faith.

As we begin this second chapter on faith, my prayer is that by the time we close this chapter, we will all be living the faith. In Luke 18:8 Jesus asks, "When the Son of Man returns, will He find faith on the earth"? That Word has inspired me to study, dig out, and apply the realities and possibilities of faith.

So, the foundation of everything goes back to John 1:1, "In the beginning was the Word." The beginning of everything is the word of faith. That's the beginning of everything. That's the way God set up and established everything. We didn't set it up that way; God did. We need to live by God's Word, by God's law and principle of faith.

Let's uncover and discover more in the power of our words, our confessions, the things we say as believers in Christ. I want to weave James 1:26 into many of these teachings on faith. James, the brother of Jesus, states, "A person who claims to have religion, but has not yet learned to bridle his tongue deceives himself." Here is what I glean from that Scripture during these months of my deep dive into faith.

Our hearts are the soil that receive the seed of our words. If we're saying words in private, such as: "I'll never get well. I'll never get ahead. I'll never get out of this depression. My family will never be saved. My car will never work. I'll never excel at what I dream to be or do." Whatever words we say are like seeds. Our words are seeds that we sow into our heart and the heart of others. Our heart was created by God to receive and reproduce those seeds. So, if we say things in private, our heart believes that is what we want. Then, when we walk into public settings, if we say things that we think will help people, then our heart is deceived, because it is getting two messages. Therefore, I believe this is an important verse for all of us.

Sometimes when I feel down, I spout flippant words I should not. I surely should not speak flip or glib stuff. We should learn to speak over our lives only words that God speaks about us and others. We should not speak words over us or them that Satan speaks. To be clear, we should speak over our marriages, our families, our ministries, our business, our cities, our nation, and the world only words that God speaks about us and them. I will probably weave that reality into every one of these chapters, because I think it's so important, vital, essential.

We don't need to be spiritually schizophrenic. We don't want to be divided or to deceive our hearts. We need to speak one consistent way all the time. Let's learn to talk like Jesus, to declare words all the time the way the Lord speaks and wants us to speak. That is the overflow of the heart being filled by the reality, substance, and power of the Word of God.

I will give you an example of something I said one morning as we were waiting for more than 70 leaders and intercessors to login into an online Zoom gathering. I said, "I wish I had Dave's metabolism." Okay: it sounds funny; you know, he's thin! That sounds like a good statement, but those were not words from the Lord. Instead, my words with God's faith substance would be, "I have the power of the resurrection inside my body, waiting to change my metabolism."

I want improvements in my words like that revelation and truth. I trudge a long, long way to get there sometimes. Do you know what I mean? Over time, our spirit and soul or heart will receive the seeds of our words and start to reproduce them. If most of what our hearts receive is the same kind of negative, critical, cynical, doubtful words I speak, then...do I make myself clear? No always, because Christ and I want my words to be like Him, accurate and transparent.

For example, not long ago, I woke up one night praying for two men who are partners with Becoming Love Ministries. The Lord took me on an imaginary journey with them. We three men were walking together through fields somewhere. It was similar to the scene in

*Gladiator* when he was getting ready to die, walking through the field waving his hands over the wheat. One of these partners walking with me was touching a harvest with his hands and releasing the power of Christ. I started to pray for those men with words from the Holy Spirit through my spirit that were reproducing the power of the Lord in them. I want to live that reality always.

Now, let's continue in John 6:63, "It is the Spirit who gives life. The flesh provides no benefit. The words that I have spoken to you are spirit and life." God's Word is Spirit. And the Spirit gives us life. So, when I confess and agree with God's Word, His Word transmits images to my mind. Words we speak actually describe our thoughts and reality moment by moment.

Remember, and I repeat: we say what we believe in most moments. That's what we say. If we say, "I'm really struggling and this is so hard, so discouraging," that's what we believe in that moment. Our words always express what we believe. By contrast, when we declare God's Word, He creates images in our mind that generate faith patterns that we start believing. This is why Solomon wrote in Proverbs 23:7, "As a person thinks within herself or himself, so she or he is." Our thoughts conceive images in our minds, which establish belief patterns and words. Then, those actualize the life we will live, what we become, and what we keep speaking.

In Ephesians 3:20, Paul writes "God is able to do more than we can ask or imagine." I think God wants our belief to explode in imagination. God can do more than we can ask or imagine! And all of this is according to His power that works within us. I think His power working within us is directly tied to the measure of faith we receive from Him, speak with words, and put into practice.

I believe we've all been given a measure of faith. Romans 12:3 reminds us that every person has been given a measure of faith. But if faith

## NOW FAITH!

comes by hearing the word of Christ, then the measure of faith each of us think, speak, and practice results from how much of the Word of Christ we are actually hearing and believing.

Further, I believe if we are determined to plant more of the Word images into our minds, then images from the world will hold less and less influence over our hearts. I'll give you a case study. One night recently, we invited our family to our home. We were playing Rook and eating leftovers. Later, I started to watch TV news.

By the time I watched an hour of that day's news cycle, I felt depressed. I felt discouraged. I felt slimed. I felt like we are in the end times: global pandemic, depression, suicide, bad weather, wars, rumors of wars, earthquakes, and famines. Why did I fill my mind with an hour of news? Really? This is not funny! It's serious, distressing, and far too common for many of us, including me.

The next day, I spent seven hours listening to the Bible. Then, I was finishing study through the whole Bible for the 24th time this year. These past few days, I have been listening seven to eight hours a day. And what results? I am going to explode with faith and the Word. So, this is amazing: we can invest seven hours being encouraged in the Word, but one hour can zap it when we listen to the narrative of the world.

Listen carefully. We must pay attention to the words we speak and words we hear and words we allow into our minds. Why? Because all of these create images, then images create thoughts, then thoughts create belief, and belief creates our reality. I want to learn to guard my heart. I want to learn to guard my tongue. I want to learn to help other people guard their hearts and tongues also. So help me and us together, Jesus!

Therefore, I will not accept things into me that I do not want roaring out of me. I want to tear down every word spoken into my life that does not align with the Word of God. Does that make sense? I don't want one weapon formed against me that would destroy an opportunity to flourish for the Lord. I want to rip every word out by the roots, if it doesn't line up with what God's Word says about me.

Again, our words describe our reality. Here's another example. If our body is susceptible to disease or distress, and all we ever say and feel about our body is, "This old bod is terrible. It never feels well or works right. It always breaks down." Well then, we are probably going to keep feeling terrible, sick, in pain, and stressed. Why? Because our thoughts, feelings, and words have power.

God created everything with words. He put his nature in us. He put His Word in us. So, why wouldn't we arrest feeling and affirm faith instead, "By trusting in the Word and the Lord, my body is going to feel well and work right. My body is going to be blessed more and stressed less. By faith, I am not going to keep breaking down. By the Holy Spirit's power in me, I will live fruitful and fulfilled as long as the Lord gives me breath." Why wouldn't we choose to use words of faith that express potential to create that reality, instead of saying so often words based on what we're feeling or seeing? This is the fight of faith!

We remember when John the Baptist was locked up in prison, his last stent for saying what he did to the king. His words with questioning were generated by his circumstances, "Ask Jesus if He is really the Messiah." Those words were not from his spirit. Those were not words from his heart. He knew Jesus was the Messiah.

Then, he lost his head. Literally, right? We need to think, decide, and speak words out of the overflow of the heart filled by the reality of God's Word. We need to choose not to speak out of the overflow of real pressures from this world or their words. We can choose. We can guard our tongue and tone. Amen?

## NOW FAITH!

I remember one time I was driving my Suburban in Dallas to preach a revival. It was a new Suburban: I only had it for about a month. I remember it was hot in the Metroplex, about 110 degrees. Suddenly, my air conditioner broke. On top of that, I was driving to my hotel on a Saturday to start a meeting Sunday morning. And I thought, "I can't do this. I'm dying." I powered windows down, because it was almost like a furnace. The vehicle was hot, and I was hotter. It was like a furnace blowing hot air in my car. Again, I thought, "I am going to die."

So, I pulled over and called a bunch of dealerships, but no service department was open because it was Saturday afternoon. I pulled into a Shell station and parked in a shady spot. I said, "Okay, this is crazy, but I'm going to do it." It was too hot to put my hands on the hood of the car because it was burning. So, I put them on the dash of my car inside. And I spoke right to my air conditioner.

I declared, "Air conditioner, you need to work now. You're too young, you're too new to ever break down, you should never break down again. I command you to work, I need you to work because I am on assignment for God. I don't have time for this."

I drove to a gas pump, filled the fuel, and started my car. The air conditioner never stopped working again as long as I owned that vehicle. Now, I'm wondering what could happen when we choose to speak only words coming from what God's Word says. When we do all things through Christ who strengthens us, then nothing is impossible for the one who believes.

I don't think we begin to tap into the power of faith. I know I haven't. Often, I am more comfortable doing things based on what I know I can do. But the Lord comes through when we do whatever He tells us to do, like Jesus' mother Mary spoke quietly and confidently, "Okay, guys, do whatever Jesus tells you to do."

I want to get to the place where I practice every time whatever the Word says. I rely on the Lord alive in me to help me, because I know God will do whatever He promises or purposes in His Word. I don't need to think long or negotiate with Him. Just speak the truth! Amen?

So, where does faith come from so we can declare God's Word? Note Romans 10:17, "Faith comes by hearing, and hearing by the words of Christ." Words. Words of Messiah. Listen to this. His words describe His reality; our words describe our reality. Words either transmit fear, or they transmit faith. Again, the words we speak either transmit fear--which grows unbelief, doubt, and worry--or they transmit faith, which grows possibilities that are unlimited through the Word of God. Those are two realities of what our words do.

Now, let's consider 2 Corinthians 4:13, "...having the same spirit of faith, according to what is written." Look at that. Remember in Romans 3, we talked about the principle of faith "having the same spirit of faith according to what is written." So, this is not a rote methodology regarding the law and principle of faith. This is a reality and a way to practice living: we actually put more trust in what the Word says, than in what our circumstances indicate and argue. This spirit of faith is based totally and consistently on what is written in the Word of God.

Now, according to Revelation 19:10, "The spirit of prophecy is the testimony of Jesus." So, it's not about mostly about foretelling the future. The spirit of prophecy is telling the truth, receiving and speaking words of knowledge, living prophetically. That is the outcome of a reality and a way of life in the Spirit of Christ.

So, when we say, "the spirit of faith", we mean the nature and the essence of faith. What does that look like and how does that play out? The next phrase answers, "I believe, therefore, I spoke. We believe; therefore, we also speak." So, the spirit of faith flows from the

# NOW FAITH!

Lord into each of us individually. If we really believe this, then faith will influence those around us. Then faith becomes corporate and we experience the dynamic power of agreement, unity, harmony!

Let's read Romans 8:2, "For the law of the Spirit of life in Christ Jesus has set you free from the law of sin and death." Now, compare that to what Jesus taught in John 6:63, "The Spirit gives life, and the words I speak to you are Spirit." Again, "Faith comes by hearing, and hearing by the words of Christ."

This is the law or the spirit of faith that flows into what is written. That spirit of faith changes what we believe, and our mouth speaks out of the overflow of our heart. So, what is this again? Romans 8:2, "The law of the Spirit of life" is the law of faith. Because God's Word is Spirit, our the words flow from our spirit. The more we release this principle and practice of faith, the more we live in Christ's Kingdom realm, right? Because "The kingdom of God is not a matter of eating or drinking, but it is righteousness, peace, and joy in the Holy Spirit" (Romans 14:17).

The more of God's Word we speak, the more of His Spirit we release. The more of His Spirit we release, the greater the realm and reign of the Kingdom we live in. And our words, therefore, end up producing the life we're living. "We live off the fruit of our lips" (Proverbs 18:20). So, we should declare righteousness: right relationships, right teaching, and right words. We should not sit under or tolerate or agree with wrong teaching or wrong words.

Faith does not make God do one thing. Faith is the component or avenue that allows us to align with what God's Word says that He has already done or will do. Faith doesn't force God to do one thing. We should not try to strong-arm God and pressure him to do anything. Faith enables us to receive everything He has already done. When we get our spirit in line with His Word, which is His Spirit, then the two become one and everything His Word does is fulfilled in our reality.

Faith requires a bending. In the 1904 Welsh Revival when Evan Roberts was age 26, he cried out, "Bend me, Lord!" The law of faith, the spirit of faith, the law of life, and the spirit of life are transforming our carnal-mind, soul-mind, our natural-mind. We are transformed from needing verification by "I will believe it when I see it" into so much more. "Now, I believe it because the Lord is bending me by the reality of God's Word into alignment and unity with the Word of the Lord, the Spirit of Jesus. This is holiness. This is not "name it and claim it." This is God spoke it. I want to live it. I will live it.

Faith is the ability to receive and conceive God's Word and carry His words to full term and full practice. Read this aloud again: **faith is the ability to receive and conceive God's Word and carry His words to full term and full practice.** This is where some people give up on faith because they don't know how long the process will take until the seed of the Word in them produces a new birth and a holy human heart and whole human life. This is the dilemma of faith: it is always too soon to quit. Faith is the ability to receive and conceive God's Word.

Let's look at Luke 1:12-17. "Zechariah was troubled when he saw the angel and fear gripped him. But the angel said to him, 'Do not be afraid, Zechariah, for your prayer has been heard. Your wife Elizabeth will bear you a son. You shall name him John. You will have joy and gladness and many will rejoice over his birth. For he will be great in the sight of the Lord. And He will drink no wine or liquor and he will be filled with the Holy Spirit while still in his mother's womb. He will turn many of the sons of Israel back to the Lord their God. And it is he who will go as a foreigner before him in the spirit and power of Elijah to turn the hearts of fathers back to their children, the disobedient

## NOW FAITH!

to the attitudes of the righteous, to make ready a people prepared for the Lord.'"

There is more in the last words of verse 17 than we will ever know this side of eternity. Most of us get tripped up on proper timing. We stagger from the reality of initial faith compared with faith that is manifested now. So, in the natural, few of us question the power of God when He visibly or audibly manifests His power and glory. But most people like us and others tend to question the power of God when faith is in seed form or just starting to sprout.

Let's continue in verse 18: "Zechariah said to the angel, 'How will I know this? For I'm an old man and my wife has advanced in her years.' The angel answered and said to him, 'I am Gabriel, who stands in the presence of God, and I was sent to speak to you and to bring you this good news. Now, you will be silent and unable to speak, until the day when these things take place, because you did not believe my words, which will be fulfilled at their proper time."

What was wrong with Zechariah? He questioned the Word of God. He wasn't willing to receive and conceive and carry the Word of the Lord full term or full practice.

This leads us to an important truth. All the promises in the New Covenant from God are conditional. They are not merely clear, open promises. All the LORD's promises are conditional. What does that mean? We need to believe them. We need to believe and obey.

We are never wrong to question how God is going to do something, especially when we don't understand. But we are never right to question God Himself. He is Truth and He cannot lie. He sees everything from the realm of faith. Much of the time we barely and merely see from the realm of the natural. Then, as we become more like Jesus and begin to see from the realm of faith, we will experience less and less difficulty to trust God for what seems impossible to us.

Everything He does starts with the Word, which is faith in substance, essence, and practice. That's the beginning of faith. Faith always comes by hearing: matter hears, mountains hear, weather hears, seasons hear, angels hear, economies hear, and ears hear. Everything starts with the Word. God operates from the realm of faith. When we align with the spirit of faith, we will experience less disconnect between what God is saying, and what we are willing to agree, say, and do. Amen?

Let's look at the contrast between Zechariah and Mary, beginning in Luke 1:26. "Now in the sixth month, the angel Gabriel was sent from God to a city in Galilee called Nazareth, to a virgin betrothed to a man whose name was Joseph, of the descendants of David. And the virgin's name was Mary. And coming in, he said to her, 'Greetings, favored one, the Lord is with you.' But she was very perplexed at this statement and was pondering what kind of greeting this was.

"Then, the angel said to her, 'Do not be afraid, Mary. You have found favor with God. And you will conceive in your womb and give birth to a son, and you shall name his name Jesus. He will be great and will be called the Son of the Most High. The Lord God will give Him the throne of His father David. He will reign over the house of Jacob forever, and His Kingdom will have no end.'

"But Mary said to the angel, 'How will this be since I am a virgin?'" See, she didn't understand. She was never questioning God. She was merely questioning, "'How can this happen? I am a virgin.' The angel answered her, 'The Holy Spirit will come on you and the power of the Most High will overshadow you. And for that reason, the Holy Child will be called the Son of God.'"

# NOW FAITH!

Let's pause here for just a minute. What is one of the main reasons the Holy Spirit wants to "overshadow" all of us and baptize all of us? What God is saying will become the reality of what we are willing to say. Perhaps that is the true purpose of the baptism with the Spirit: a personal power that "overshadows" and fills our whole being so dynamically and continually that we fully believe now and we say now what God is saying. Then, He fulfills it now!

Let's continue with verses 35-37: "The Holy Spirit will come on you and the power of the Most High will overshadow you. And for that reason, the Holy Child will be called the Son of God. And even your relative Elizabeth herself has conceived a son in her old age, and she was called infertile. She is now six months pregnant, for nothing will be impossible with God."

When someone on earth agrees with God's conditions, that is the principle of faith in practice. God would not have forced Mary to become pregnant. We need to hear this. The Lord is not going to force healing on any one of us. He's not going to force freedom or influence or peace or prosperity on any of us. He won't force feed His seed to any of us. But He is waiting on all of us to agree with it. And come in line with it, so we can receive it. Do you hear what I'm saying?

Now, let's look at verse 38: "But Mary said, 'Behold the Lord's bond-servant." She said, "I'll be your love-servant, Lord. Whatever God wants is exactly what I want." And God wasn't even Jesus in the flesh yet. But the LORD was certainly a Person who was personal enough she could talk to. "Behold the Lord's bondservant. May this be done unto me according to your word. Then the angel left her."

Mary received and believed and conceived the Word of God. The rest is history. Her confession became her seed. Her profession lined up with what God's Word said. And her seed crushed the head of Satan. Is that good news? Amen!

Won't it be amazing when by faith all of our confessions crush the head of satan in our life? What kind of lifestyle will that be? When everything we say makes it painfully hard for satan to exist in our presence! I would love to live a life through which every word coming out of my mouth is from the Word of God, and through which every word makes Satan's existence extremely painful and discouraging. I want to live my life that way. I don't want to say words that make him comfortable hanging around me. I want to say words that make him miserable around me. Are you with me?

Let's illustrate with an airplane. My daddy, Jim Bohi, had two planes when he started to travel in evangelism way back in the late 1960's and early 70's until about 1974. He flew until the wings iced up one time and he couldn't maintain altitude. He thought he was going to die. Then, he sold his planes. I never flew with him because I was young, but he flew until he thought he would die, then he sold them. Here is why I think his experience flying is important.

Faith in the law of lift is a reality. The law of lift has to do with the amount of thrust that allows the law of aerodynamics to work. So, we have thrust, we have lift, and we have aerodynamics. Got it? My dad told me several times he knew mom prayed faithfully for him at home because he didn't have instrument rating. So, when he flew sometimes in fog, he flew low enough to see cities, landmarks, and highways.

I don't like stories my dad tells about flying. I like to sit in first class and not worry about all the laws of aerodynamics. Thrust results when you hit the throttle. Thrust depends on horsepower. I compare thrust to confession. Lift is what happens when thrust creates aerodynamics. The more thrust, the faster the plane flies. The wing is designed so that with more thrust and speed, less air goes over the wing and more air is pushed under the wing. The result is lift.

So, thrust illustrates our confession. Lift is how faith works. Wing design is how our heart is created. The Lord designed us to go from glory to glory. We were not created to live like the lyrics in a country western song: one step forward and two steps back. That's not how God created us. He actually created us to go from faith to faith, righteousness to righteousness, glory to glory, and truth to truth.

So, you and I confess the Word of God, right? For instance, "I believe and receive that my body is healed. I believe my family will be saved. I believe my church will grow. I believe my ministry or business will prosper." We confess the Word. We confess what God's Word says. That's thrust. The more we confess, the faster we will move and grow in the Spirit realm.

God's Word moves at the speed of Presence. We need to hear this. His Word does not move at the speed of light. Rather, God's Word produced light. God can be everywhere all at once and His Word moves at the speed of His Presence. So, the more we confess the Word, the more our heart, the wing, is enabled to start soaring. From glory to glory, higher and higher.

Lift is how faith works. When I look back on my life, I notice seasons of lift and faith. During those seasons, I saw the Lord bring the most people to be born again and the most persons to be baptized in the Spirit. Also, I saw the most people healed of depression, cancer, paralysis, and other desperations. Those were the seasons that I was most actively confessing realities of faith in the Lord. While writing these chapters on faith, I realize that when I confess and believe the Word the most, I soar in Spirit realms of lift the most. I receive from the Lord the most thrust, which creates the most lift, which enables me to ascend the highest.

The higher we are in faith, the more authority and dominion we have over circumstances. If we actually believe we are seated above all the things we are commanding to move, then faith works easier from above than from below. Do you perceive that word picture?

Here's what happens to us. Sometimes, we start cruising and we see God moving. Suddenly, we don't feel a need to confess so much anymore. We can save energy. We can save fuel. We can focus on something different. Then, we pull back the throttle and we slow down, right? Then, we say, "So, well, that worked okay."

We assume we can save a little more fuel. We pull it back a little more and we slow down a little more. Well, here's the danger. If we pull back our confession too much, we no longer have any thrust. If we don't have any thrust, the only principle that makes the wing work is falling. That is how major airliners land: they slow the thrust down enough and the descent allows the airplane to land on a runway.

So, I propose that if we never stop confessing the Word of God, we will have an unending supply of thrust, an incomprehensible amount of lift, and there will be nothing impossible to the ones who believe. Are we hearing and receiving this?

Listen carefully: our confession of the Word is the throttle for our lift and thrust. Mary conceived the Word because she confessed the truth God spoke to her. Then, the Truth manifested in her physical body. That conception was through an act of a God-Present-faith that could not be explained in natural terms. She expressed 100% trust and belief in a supernatural realm that can only be supernaturally discerned.

We know multiple examples throughout the Bible of this kind of Mary faith. Do you remember when the Spirit of the LORD asked

# NOW FAITH!

Ezekiel, "Can these bones live?" There was no way in the natural they could live, was there! There was no way.

Do you remember when Moses asked God, "How am I supposed to provide water for these people?" The LORD responded, "Just hit the rock." There's no way that works in the natural realm, right? Come on!

Also, Jesus said to His disciples, "Throw your nets in the water and pull whatever comes up. Then, you can pay your taxes." There's no way that works in the natural realm. Do you get it?

There are thousands of similar examples in the Bible: people trusted the Word of God, and their faith allowed the unseen supernatural reality to become their reality. The manifested realm of the senses is part of the law of faith. The miracle realm of the supernatural is part of the law of faith.

So, Mary heard, then believed, then received, then confessed God's Word, and then practiced what the Bible teaches. Faith comes by hearing. Now what are we going to do to believe? Are we going to let faith become our reality?

Can we say it and repeat it? "I hear the Word, I believe the Word, I receive the Word, I confess the Word, and I practice the Word." Or are we merely going to say, "Well, that was a good thing for somebody else, but that can never happen for me." If you say that, you just talked yourself out of now faith. Why? Because every word is a seed that produces a harvest.

Let's look at Matthew 4:4 where Jesus answered it and said, "It is written. Man shall not live on bread alone, but on every word that comes out of the mouth of God." Now Jesus said that we live on every word. Again, faith comes by hearing, and hearing by every word. In essence, He is saying we live by faith.

That is also what Habakkuk and Paul wrote: "The righteous or just will live by faith." Because faith comes by hearing, and hearing comes by the word, then we live on every word. So, life is in The Voice. Come on! Life is in The Voice of the Lord by the Spirit and through the Word.

In Galatians chapter three, Paul asked that congregation, "Why are you struggling and trying so much to go back to the law instead of staying in faith?" Isn't that a danger for all of us? Do you know why churches lose the spirit of power and glory and miracles? They go back to the law instead of staying in the spirit of faith. Isn't that the sequence?

Historians among us know that from the time of Jesus, the Orthodox Church and the Catholic Church kept track of orders or cycles of revival we call denominations. These started by believing the Word. Then, many went back to what they could do in the flesh. Even today, they keep adding to the Word and then they die.

That's the cycle. That's the battle. Do we live in faith by believing the Word and doing what the Word says? Or do we add our own words and ideas? That's the cycle. Then, they usually have a life cycle of 70 to 150 years.

The LORD intends to start a new cycle of people who hear the Word and believe that is enough and all. Paul writes in Galatians 3:5, "This is God who works miracles among you and gives you the Holy Spirit." Does he do this by works of the law, or through faith that comes by hearing? We're talking about genuine faith. There is more power in one word of God, than all the words the world produces. There's more power in one word of God.

Let's look at Genesis 2:7. "God formed man of the dust from the ground and breathed into his nostrils the breath of life. And man became a

# NOW FAITH!

living person." That sounds like Matthew 4:4, "Men and women do not live on bread alone, but on every word." In the beginning, how was humanity formed? By the word of God, His breath. His Word is Spirit and His Spirit brings life.

If we are living in the Word, confessing the Word, and speaking the Word, we're speaking the Spirit. When we're speaking the Spirit, we're speaking life! I want to live fulness of life. I don't want to live under the law of death and condemnation. I want to live in the Spirit that brings life to every area. Listen: our spirits die if we don't receive the Spirit's life in the Word of God.

Here is another way to look at this. Many people fall away, quit living by faith, and quit gathering with other believers in the Body of Christ. Then, they give up on God and everything unravels. Do you know how this normally begins? They pulled back on the throttle. They stopped studying the Word daily. They could no longer stay aloft and alive.

Many persons in many situations who used to be on fire for God are now not even in relationship with God. They just walked away. That does not mean God walked away. It means they chose to walk away. God remains forever and His Word remains forever. He wants to finish everything He started in every one of us in whom He started His own good work in the Word. He has not changed His mind just because we changed our minds. But it often starts with, "Well, I've been there and done that. It doesn't work for me! It's just too hard. Nobody understands. I'm just too broken. I'll never get ahead. I'll never get my miracle. I'm so tired of hearing everybody else's stories." Not one of those comes from the Word of God. Our words create a harvest. Eventually, we believe either our words or His Word.

In John 6:63 Jesus teaches, "All the words I speak are spirit." And the Spirit brings life. It was Mary's seed that agreed with God's Word. That spirit of faith made John 1:14 a reality: "And the Word became flesh."

Now, if this faith will work in Mary, will it work in us? Yes! The Word of God produced Christ in Mary, and our confession of the Word will allow Christ to manifest in our mortal flesh. He has not changed: He is the same yesterday, today, and forever. He is waiting on us to confess His Word, to believe Him enough to say it, not merely think about it. We actually declare it. We actually say it, "I'm healed. I'm free. I'm blessed." That is what it takes for Christ to manifest.

For any believer who will receive God's Word for personal needs, God will produce and manifest what His Word promises. For any believer who is covered by the promises that are multiplied in the New Testament, God will produce and manifest what His Word promises. And for any believer who allows God's Word (seed) to conceive in spiritual womb or their heart, God will produce and manifest what His Word promises. God cannot lie. God's Word is true. His Word cannot lie. Period. His Word is good seed that will produce a bountiful harvest in us!

"God's Word is seed" (1 Peter 1:23). It doesn't go bad. In Genesis 3:15, the LORD spoke a seed in the Garden of Eden, "The woman's seed will crush your head." When He said it, and His Word became her seed, that seed still had life to produce what God said.

Some of us have been struggling with some issue or concern for 5 years, 10 years, even 20 years. Remember, God's seed lasted 4,000 years and it still worked. I'm trying to encourage you. None of us is going to live 4,000 years in these bodies. So, none of us have to worry about that. Instead, we must keep confessing. Keep the thrust going. Keep the throttle down. Keep believing enough to speak the Word of God until we believe it. According to 2 Corinthians 4:13, "We believe; therefore, we speak!"

In Luke 1:37, the Word reminds us, "All things are possible with God." Then, Mary responded, "Behold the Lord's bondservant. Let it be done to me according to your Word."

## NOW FAITH!

Instead, some say doubt-filled words such as, "Well, that's okay, but I am broke." Look at Luke 6:38, "Give and it will be given to you. They will pour into your lap a good measure, pressed down, shaken together, and running over. For by your standard of measure, it will be measured to you in return." Why don't we believe and speak that instead of, "I am broke"?

Let's believe the Word. So, what does this look like? I invite you to enter now into an experiment I have entered. Let's covenant to create a better, fuller, life by the words we confess on a daily basis.

Not long ago, for some reason I had extreme pain in my body that was more than normal. I was susceptible to negative phrases coming out of my mouth. Has anyone else ever been tempted to speak negative phrases? Let's be honest with the Lord and ourselves.

Finally, I mentioned previously that I will show you how the Lord's working in my life to confirm truth. As I started a recent year, the Lord challenged me to study through the Bible 24 times. So, when I completed what He said, I wrote this confession on the very last page of my journal. I had written all my calendar dates: communion, study Bible 88 pages daily, holiday resting, Zoom meetings, healing services, prayer room, etc. I had one page left to write my confession of faith. I want to give you an example of what I decided to do every day in my new annual journal. I challenge you to practice and live this also. Are you with me?

"Heavenly Father. The pain in my body has increased all year. However, I will continue to stand and declare your Word: By your stripes, I was healed. You have carried my pain. You came to bind up the brokenhearted. You sent your Word and healed and saved me. Those who find your Word find life and health for all their bones. Yes, these bones can live again! Yes, this mountain of pain will move. Yes, this tree of affliction will be uprooted and cast into the sea. I will live in abundant life and declare the glory of Christ in the land of the living. I will prosper and be in good health, even as my soul prospers. I will be blessed in my going, in my resting, in my coming, in my ministry, and the coming new year will be the greatest year I have ever experienced. Because my eyes are fixed on you. I love you, Jesus. Thank you for loving me and dying for me. Your servant, Dan."

Can you imagine how I felt after I wrote that out with faith and repeated it out loud in faith? I felt like a different person. Not by feelings, but by faith in the Word of God.

If we choose to confess by faith what God's Word says over our lives daily, we can hardly imagine what the Lord would accomplish in each of us by the end of each year. That's my challenge to you. I choose. And I challenge you to create God's reality in your life by believing His Word enough to confess it aloud daily over yourself. What do you think about that?

Some might say, "Well, that sounds crazy." No, I believe this actually sounds biblical. What if all we ever say about ourselves is what God says about us! He might change our lives! Could He change our lives? Amen? May it be, by God's grace through faith in His Word.

# 3
# BELIEVING WHAT GOD HAS ALREADY DONE

As we continue learning how to live by faith, let's review several motives for this focus. First, in Luke 18:8 Jesus asks, "When the Son of Man returns, will He find faith on the earth?" I want Him to find faith in you, everyone globally, and me. We're not the only ones, but we are a small group of people totally committed to living real faith in Jesus Christ.

Second, I am compelled to write on faith because we will need to live the faith more and more as the days become increasingly challenging. I think we're going to see global, spiritual and moral erosion and experience challenges we have never imagined. We need to be rooted and grounded in faith. I am excited about the possibilities of living in faith.

Third, the Lord is training you and me by faith for new ministries that will become more effective during end times. We will capture the hearts of next generations while we affirm biblical truth for a thousand generations. God speaks all the time. It's up to His sheep, His bride, His Body, His family, to hear what He is saying in the present. Only He can give us the courage to say it. The true Body of Messiah is learning to balance and declare truth that is old and new, that is both Word and Spirit. What we live and teach among next generations should always affirm and never negate what He said in the past. By faith, we will be able to apply what He said then and is saying now. Now faith!

So now, let's continue in Mark 4:26 where Jesus taught, "The kingdom of God is like a man who casts seed upon the soil. And he goes to bed at night and gets up daily, and the seed sprouts and grows. How that happens he does not know. The soil produces the crops all by itself. First the stalk, then the head, then the mature grain."

On this same day Jesus taught 13 parables, all of which described the relationship between seed and soil. Earlier in Mark 4, Jesus said, "If you can understand this, you will understand everything I teach." You and I are the only ones who can sow our seed. Nobody else can sow our seed. If seeds are going to be planted in our heart from our mouth, we will have to do it. God is not sowing seeds. He is waiting on us to sow seeds.

Jesus says the kingdom is like a man or a woman. The kingdom is not like God dumping it out of heaven. We need to be planting the seeds. If we're planting seeds that are good, we should never give up on a harvest. God designed our hearts to produce automatically what we put in them. So, let's make sure we're putting good seeds in our heart. Right?

We're talking about living the faith. Let's refuse to plant seeds of fear, worry, and anxiety in our hearts. Let's plant what the Word of God says about us in our hearts. Let's confess the Word daily, meditate on the Word daily, contemplate the Word daily, memorize the Word daily, listen to and live the Word daily. Let's plant seeds that produce the harvest we want. Come on! What we want is the substance of our faith.

Mark 11:23 is how this works, "Truly I say to you, whoever says to this mountain, be taken up and thrown into the sea, and does not doubt in his heart, but believes that what he says is going to happen. It will be granted to him." This is how the law of faith works. We can have what we say if we believe the Word, speak the Word, and believe what we say.

Jesus established faith that way. He said we can have what we say if it aligns with His Word, and we believe in our heart that what we say will happen. I don't know of any scenario that will work unless we know we are saying what the Word of God says. It cannot be merely what we want. It must be what God is wanting from the beginning. When what we say agrees with what God says, it becomes what we want. Then, we agree with God and that's a big majority. Again, the law of faith works this way. When our faith is in the Lord and His Word, let's say it, pray it, believe it, receive it, and thank the Lord for it.

Some people say to me, "Well, I've been declaring for three weeks, and nothing has changed." So, it's not automatic, like if we say it, it's going to happen automatically. However, here is what will happen automatically: our faith will start agreeing and our heart will start believing what we say. That will happen automatically.

The timing of harvest always depends on God. We cannot control the harvest, but we can control planting the seed in good soil of our hearts. We can control how many times we water that seed and how many times we fertilize that seed. You and I can control that; we can do our part. God's part is grace; our part is faith. Grace through faith will only work with God's part and our part together. Saying what we believe is essential and speaking faith is how it works automatically. Come on! God plants it in our mouth so He and we can move it into our heart.

Not long ago, I was invited into a meeting of 17 leaders collaborating to archive the largest collection of biblical archaeological artifacts into a museum. We also discussed what's happening on the world scene. And recently, more than a million intercessors around the world focused three weeks in passionate prayer with fasting. What is unfolding right now has never happened in the history of the world. So much is unprecedented. We are going to have to learn to live by faith. I cannot reiterate this enough.

Some of what I write is review, and some of this will be new for you. We are discovering principles or laws of faith. Together, let's learn faith in 1,000 different ways. I pray at least one of these will stick.

I illustrate: one night during recent holidays, our daughter-in-law invited our whole family to their home for spaghetti. When she was cooking the pasta, she asked our granddaughter Kaylee to grab a string and throw it on the wall. If the string stuck on the wall, it was ready to eat! Likewise, I'm hoping that one of these teachings will stick in your heart, ready for you to devour and to become your reality. I'm trying to describe "faith-ing" adequately in multiple biblical ways so that eventually some will stick. Does that make sense?

Now, let's look at Genesis 1:11. "Then God said, 'Let the earth sprout vegetation: plants yielding seed and fruit trees on the earth bearing fruit according to their kinds with seed in them. The earth produced vegetation plants, yielding seed according to their kind, and trees bearing fruit with seeds in them according to their kind. And God saw that it was good."

So, what's the point? This is God's method for everything we will ever need on the earth. Everything we will ever need already has the seed in itself. God's Word and our words are seeds. So, everything we say also has the ability to reproduce. That is the way God made it. If we sow love, we will reap love. If we sow faith, we will reap belief. If we sow finance, we will reap favor and blessing. If we sow what the Bible says about health, we will reap healing. Why? Because good seed produces after its kind: more good seed. This is a law that the LORD put in place in the beginning of human history. The seed is in itself.

Now, we consider Luke 17:3-6 where Jesus taught, "Be on your guard. If your brother sins, rebuke him. If he repents, forgive him. If he sins against you seven times in a day and returns you seven times saying, 'I repent,' you shall forgive him. The apostles said to the Lord, 'Increase our faith.' But the Lord said, 'If you have faith the size of a mustard seed, you can say to this mulberry tree, 'Be uprooted and planted in the sea', and it would obey." The disciples thought they needed more faith. Jesus said, No, you just need to use your measure of tiny faith you have until it becomes mighty faith.

We will never plant a seed until we believe it's a seed. If we think it's a theory and if we say, "Oh, that's only what Dan or Jim or Melissa says", then it's a theory, a theology, a doctrine. But when it becomes our reality, then it becomes a seed. That's when we should plant it.

In Genesis 8:22, the Word teaches, "As long as there is day and night, cold and winter, summer and warm, there is seedtime and harvest." I love that. We have the ability to control our destiny, as long as we are willing to plant seed, which will always produce a harvest of what it is, after its own kind. So, if we need peace, we need to plant some peace, give some peace, carry some peace, with seeds of peace.

One afternoon recently, I met with 25 businesspeople from San Francisco who have issues, problems, and pain. So, with faith in the Word and Spirit of the Lord, we offered inner healing and hope for them. We planted Good News seeds by faith. I threw many seeds of comfort that I knew would transform them. Seed faith always produces what we plant. The seed is always good if it comes from the Word.

I know Jesus said that only a fourth of the hearts are ready to receive it. I get it. I'm not the one trying to pick and choose which hearts are ready. I just want to keep sowing good seeds. I want to live the faith. Do you want to live the faith? Amen! We don't need more faith. We need to understand how a seed works and plant it.

Here is my question for each new challenge, each new opportunity, each new year. Do we have faith to plant the seed for what we desire? Do we really have faith for a healed home, a healed body, a healed ministry, and healed finances? Do we really have faith? Do we believe that if we could get a seed of what we desire in our heart, then God's Word would really produce what it says? Do we have faith? Do we believe enough to plant it? Like, this is only the third chapter, but this is our chance. We might not be living in the spring schedule when farmers normally plant good seed in good soil. But we can start now in real time with real faith.

The whole Bible, the Word is full of good seed. There is so much seed we could plant. If we actually believe the seed enough to plant it, we could almost reproduce heaven on earth. That's how Jesus describes His desire for our prayer life...on earth as it is in heaven. He's waiting on us to claim faith so that His Kingship and Kingdom can grow.

So, what are we declaring? What kind of faith-seed have we been planting since we completed chapters 1 and 2? If we've been declaring the Word, did we write out our desires? I'm going to describe my declarations. I created my list of hopes first: priorities I'm hoping for. Then, I started declaring the Word to immerse everything I was hoping for in God's promises about each hope. Why did I do that? Because the Bible is full of the Word. It is the Word of God, but we are the ones who have to plant it. Faith in the Word of the Lord is like a seed.

Now, here's an interesting insight: the way we plant the Word is by speaking it. That's what Jesus said in Mark 11:23-24, "You can say to

# NOW FAITH!

your mountain whatever you desire when you pray and believe." So, we can actually declare with faith, pray with faith, speak words that plant the seed. Our words plant seed: the power of words.

In James 1:8 we learn that "double-minded persons are unstable in all their ways. Now the brother or sister of humble circumstances is to glory in their high position. But the rich person is to wilt in humiliation because like flowering grass, that person will pass away. For the sun rises with its scorching heat and withers the grass. Its flowers fall off and the beauty of its appearance is destroyed. So also, the rich person in the midst of his pursuits will die out."

So, why did we put that in the middle of this? Because if we are waiting on the manifestation of the harvest to praise, we have missed the point of what it's like to live by faith. Because we don't have to possess faith for what we can see. We have to live the faith for what we are hoping for. If we're just living on what we can see, we have already left the faith. The righteousness of God is revealed from faith to faith, which means we need something bigger in our heart and in our house: that is what we are dreaming for, hoping for, and envisioning!

Faith is an "all-you-can-eat buffet", but most people take only a few bites. The meal is as big as our neighborhood. We can always enjoy as much of the Lord's nature as we're willing to receive. The more we eat, the more we will plant. We can have as much of Him as we desire.

Words have power. Recently, I noted the words of commentators on ESPN and ABC. They used to say, "We wish you well." But during a tragedy God allowed, even commentators were praying on camera, releasing words with power. That was another example of a law of faith. God illustrated a principle: when we speak words that matter, then he has something to work with. He has nothing to work with until we start speaking words with faith. His power travels in our words. That's how faith comes in.

Faith is a powerful substance. And faith needs our words to flow through. I repeat: faith needs our words, because He has already spoken His words. He is waiting on us to agree with His words. Then, the two become one. His words fit and flow through our words like a glove. Our words of faith come from His Word and His Word never returns void. Our life becomes a supernatural life from glory to glory, and righteousness to righteousness, and truth to truth, and peace to peace. Why? We never stop speaking what we're believing deep inside our heart. Why? Because His Word is all we're putting into our heart. So, our life is like an eruption of what overflows out of our heart. That's the faith!

Again, the LORD designed laws, life-principles. God spoke the law of faith into existence. For example, He spoke the law of gravity, which works in Gardner, Kansas, in Bethany, Oklahoma, in Louisville, Kentucky, in Maryland, in Nampa, and in West Virginia. Gravity works in California, in Fort Worth, in North Carolina, in Nebraska, in Tennessee, in Houston, and in Santa Maria. Gravity is a law: if you jump off a roof, you will fall.

The law of seed time and harvest is just as real as the law of gravity. The law of the Word and the law of faith are the same. If we are willing to sow and plant seeds, the law of words of faith promises to produce a harvest. God put that law into effect.

Also, think about the law of electricity. Some say, "But I can't see it." Well, they will feel it when they put their hand on a hot wire while they stand in some water. They will feel it! The principle always works when we stay within the guidelines of it.

# NOW FAITH!

Now, here's the flip side. The same law that can bless us is the law that can kill us. Proverbs 18:21 records that the power of death and life is in our tongue. And a lot of people are killing themselves by what they say, instead of producing life in themselves by what they say. The of law of faith that brings healing, deliverance, hope, joy, peace, and prosperity is the same law that reveals reasons for depression, anxiety, worry, resentment, bitterness, and entitlement.

Recently after I finished a two-hour meeting, suddenly out of nowhere, the Lord impressed on my heart that I needed to go pray for a man named Mike. What? I had heard about him, but I had never met him. I was not sure of his last name. I only knew he had a brain tumor. He lived in Lee's Summit, not far from the meeting I had finished.

So, I drove to Mike's house. When I walked in, his wife Carolyn said the timing of my coming was impeccable. That was the first day on his journey he had not been able to get out of bed. So, I went into his room and started commanding life and speaking the Word. By the time I left, it was like a different house. The brightness of the glory of God was there. Mike was shouting, "Hallelujah!" That is what faith looks like: we cannot and we do not stop sowing seed!

Do we understand? We don't wait for the harvest. We don't wait until flowers are blooming or grass is growing, or barns are overflowing. Those are not good signs in the Scripture. We need to worship when heavy chains are on us and we're in the darkest hole during the darkest part of the night. When it looks like there's no hope, then that's when faith works, because it's really faith. And that's when faith becomes a seed.

Let's gaze into Matthew 16:15-19 where Jesus asked His disciples, "Who do you say that I am?" Simon Peter answered, "You are the Christ, the Son of the living God." Then Jesus said to him, "Blessed are you, Simon bar Jonah. Flesh and blood did not reveal this to you, but my Father who is in heaven. I also say to you that you are Peter and upon this rock I will build my Church and the gates of Hades will not overpower it. I will give you the keys of the kingdom of heaven, so whatever you bind on earth shall have been bound in heaven and whatever you loose on earth shall have been loosed in heaven."

I love that, friends! When we listen to the Spirit and we say what the Spirit says, then all of a sudden, Jesus says, "Now, let Me tell you the power I have given you, because you are really believing My Word now!" What we say can loose things that are already free in heaven and what we say can bind things that aren't allowed in heaven. We access this loosing-and-binding power when we live in faith through our words. Not my words, but His Word and your words. You and I have the power of heaven in our words. We release God's power through our words and from our mouth. Our words from our mouth in the name of Jesus.

Again, Hebrews 11:1 reminds us, "Faith is the substance of things hoped for and the evidence of things we can't yet see." The substance of this powerful force called faith is based on what we're really hoping for, based on what the Word of God says is ours already...if we will really believe so we can receive it. We're not trying to conjure up something that's not been. We're trying to receive something that Jesus has already provided.

Some might say, "Well, I don't understand this." Then, let's go back to the very first page of the Bible. God created air. He created water, He created shelter, He created food, and He created plants. He created minerals, fossil fuel, electricity, and nuclear fusion. He created all the intellect there will ever be. Then, He created man. God's method: "I've got everything you need, waiting on you to believe and receive it. I don't need you to come up with it. I just need you to believe and receive what I've already done, because I'm a good father." That's the faith.

That's living the faith. He didn't create man and then Adam asked, "What am I supposed to eat?" The LORD did not respond to Adam, "Oh, right. I will create a banana." No, the LORD had already made everything. He had created everything billions of people who would ever live on this planet would ever need. He created by His words all the food ever required for the human race and its entire history, before He created man and woman.

All a farmer starts with is a seed. All God's power is in His Word, waiting to be released if we are willing to speak it. All God's power is in His Word, waiting to be released if we believe it enough to speak it and plant the seed.

Now, the same is true about evil-inspired words. That's the power producing what we call fear. In essence, fear is faith in the devil. If we have perfect faith in God, there would never be a place for fear in any of our lives. Let's repeat that right now aloud: If we have perfect faith in God, there would never be a place for fear in any of our lives. But many insist on saying, "Okay, but you know we have football players on life support. How many people died this week because of cancer? How many people died this week because of diabetes? How many people because of COVID? How many people are sex trafficked? How many people are being tortured right now? How many Christians are being abused?"

If everyone would stop believing the devil can do anything, and if everyone start believing what God says, then the devil could not replicate evil practice on this planet. All the things that we fear are only possible because we fear them. Fear is the fuel that gives the devil power and energy to operate. Fear is the enemy's number one commodity and product. If all every one of us live faith in God, we would experience no fear. Fear is faith in the devil.

If faith is the substance of things hoped for, then fear is the substance of things we don't want to happen. They both produce a harvest. Remember: faith comes by hearing. So, if we're saying words motivated by fear, they are producing faith in the devil. But if we're saying words that come from the Word of God, they are producing faith in the Lord. And what He says He will do. One produces faith, love, peace, and joy. The other produces fear, unbelief, discouragement, and anxiety. There's the great divide! It all starts with what we're saying, which comes from what we're believing.

Again, faith is the substance of what we desire and comes from hearing what God says. Fear is the substance of what we don't desire and comes from hearing what the devil says. So, we should resist fear like we resist the devil. Job said in 3:25, "What I fear comes upon me; what I dread happens to me."

So, if fear is the devil's number one tool, then fear leads to other troubles like a domino effect. We move into fear that everything the devil induced can be produced in us because that's our agreement. The moment we step into fear--whether we believe it or not, or want to acknowledge it or not--our fear is cooperating and giving the devil an access to do what he wants in our life. So, we must resist fear like we resist the devil. James 4:7 must become our lifestyle. Whenever something comes that causes fear comes, we must resist it. Resist it. Don't take on fear. We are going to declare what the Word says instead of what the devil says.

In Matthew 4:4 we read, "We don't live on bread alone, but on every word." We live on every word because faith comes by hearing and every word is a seed. And every word we hear we can plant. Again, faith comes by hearing. We live on every word, so we live by faith.

# NOW FAITH!

Remember Romans 1:17, "The righteous will live by faith." Also, "The righteousness of God has been revealed from faith to faith to faith." What sources this faith? Faith comes by hearing. By hearing what? The Word of God. If we hear it, we can say it. If we speak the Word, we're planting. And if we're planting, it is producing!

Let's read Luke 21:26, "People will be fainting, terrified with fear, apprehensive of what is coming on the world, for powers of the heavens will be shaken." This is such an essential and timely lesson for each of us! Revelation warns with even more depth that for a five month period, there's going to be so much fear in the human race, that everybody's going to cry out, "Let me die!" They are not going to be able to find death. That will be the fulfillment of satan's intention for the human race. Then, what's the antidote of fear? Now Faith! Faith in love. Faith working through love. Perfect love gets rid of all fear.

In John 6:63, Jesus says, "Flesh, profits nothing. The words that I speak are spirit, and the Spirit brings life." So, when we are saying what Jesus says, we're releasing the Spirit, and the Spirit releases life. If you have a sick loved one, speak life and health over him or her. If you have a sick bank account, speak blessing over it. You could say, "I'm going to be able to help so many people this year. I'm going to prosper and be blessed to bless others."

Do we know what limits our words? Our insecurity, our doubt in who God says we are, our fear of getting hope up in case it doesn't happen, our anxiety because of our past failures. Every one of those is a gnawing reminder from an enemy who doesn't want us to live the faith. He wants us to stay in fear. But we have hope to break out of this and change the world. What could happen if we decide by faith to change the world in our little sphere of influence? Amen!

Some say, "Well, you're preaching something that is too good to be true." But this is the gospel and it is true! So, the spirit of life is in God's Word. And the spirit of death is in the words of the devil. This is important, so let's repeat, believe, and receive. The spirit of life that brings life to our spirit is in God's Word. But the spirit of death and fear is in the words of the devil.

Let's probe an interesting verse in Proverbs 18:14, "The spirit of a person can allow him to endure in his sickness. But as for a broken spirit, no one can endure it." If we are planting God's Word in our spirit, our heart, our re-creative spirit, then even in very bad circumstances, our Spirit can sustain us!

If we embrace enough of the life of God's Word in our spirit, then no matter how much from the evil one hits our circumstances, the Spirit of the LORD in our spirit will sustain us. We will be much more than barely surviving. We will be thriving, even during assaults from darkness.

Our spirit can do whatever we put into it. I know because God designed our spirits the same way He designed soil. So, whatever we desire, we must place in our spirit. Whatever we desire, we must speak out loud. Come on! Whatever we desire, we will plant it.

We must be careful what we say! Let's weave in James 1:26 again: "A person who claims to have religion, but has not yet learned to bridle his tongue, deceives himself." What does that mean? If when we are in private, we speak things such as "I'll never have a good home. I'll never get healthy. I'll never lose weight. I'll never get ahead financially. I'll never see my kids on fire." Then, we turn around and say in public, "I'm so blessed and highly favored. God is so good. Jesus is Lord. I can't believe how much I love the Body of Christ." When our heart hears both those statements out of the same mouth, then our heart becomes deceived and dis-eased. Why? Because God designed our heart to produce what we say. So, if we talk one way in private and the opposite way in public, we practice a form of godliness without the power of the Spirit. And that powerlessness is deceiving our own heart, family, and congregation.

We need to be careful about the seeds we are planting. So, we don't pray our problems! I hear so many people praying their problems, repeating what the devil says. They are praying themselves into fear. They are praying themselves into discouragement. They are praying themselves into depression. We must stop praying our problems. We must and can start speaking the promises by faith! Pray the promises and believe!

We can pray ourselves into fear and doubt. But if we pray the Word, we can come away from a prayer time with more faith. This is real prayer: when we are finished praying, we have more faith instead of more worry. When we're done praying, we have more confidence instead of more cowardice or weakness. When we really prayed in the Spirit, we come away more energized and less burdened down with weariness in worry. If we come out of prayer wondering, "How am I going to keep going? I can't believe we have to go through this again", then we just wasted our time. We must not pray the problems. We must pray the Word. We need to control words that come out of our mouth.

Let's end this chapter with three verses. First, Psalm 138:2 where the New King James version says, "God magnifies His Word above Himself." So, we can't get a higher view: God views his Word as the highest reality. Next, we recall, "Faith comes by hearing, and hearing by the word of Christ" (Romans 10:17). Finally, we end with Mark 9:23, where Jesus asked the person struggling toward faith, "If you can? All things are possible to the one who believes."

There it is: the possibilities of faith! How can this become any clearer than Mark 9:23, "If you can." So, this is what you and I need to do. We need to sow the seed. We have to say the words. We have to believe in our heart. Faith is a gift of God, but to believe and receive is up to us. It's not up to God. He said, "It is good." The Lord Jesus declared, "It is finished." He has given all grace to all mankind who believe and receive. He has extended everything we need. Now, it's on us. If we can believe, all things are possible.

We can embrace another verse also: "If two of you agree, it will be done" (Matthew 18:19-20). Now faith affirms, "All things are possible to the one who believes" (Mark 9:23). Do we know what that promise means? I love both truths, but this verse says, "If one person will believe..." Come on! If one person will believe, a friend can be healed, a family can be set free, a neighborhood can be saved. If one will believe. God saved Nineveh! If He can save that city, then He can save Seattle! He can save Portland, Oregon! He can save Dallas! He can save Washington DC! If one person will believe, all things are possible! You say, "I don't have faith for that." What do we have faith for? What do we want? Why don't we start with our desire, declare it, and let faith grow. Let faith grow. Let faith grow.

So, as I close, I will share my confessions. In the previous chapter, I challenged us to confess the Word of God over our life daily. We want to start building a storehouse of seed going into our spiritual soil, so those seeds of faith can start producing what we are saying. That was our challenge: confess the Word of God over your life daily, right?

So, this is what I did. I wrote my hopes and commitments. I do not want to speak a rote confession that is mere methodology or a religion routine. So, this is what I wrote.

What am I hoping? I want to hear God's voice better. The Savior said, "My sheep hear My voice. Life is in My voice." I will live on His Word, His Voice. I want to move in the supernatural more than in the natural. I hope for Christ to live in me so genuinely that His Presence through me heals people, and His words through me heal people, and His touch through me sets people free.

I will illustrate again: when I came into the room to pray for that man with a brain tumor, I discerned in the Spirit that he had much more faith than his wife did. That discernment was not from me: that was in supernatural Presence beyond me. That was the Spirit of the Lord, giving me discernment that his faith was pulling on my anointing more than his wife's faith was. My faith declaration of wanting and hoping to flow in the supernatural was already manifesting.

Then, I wrote this hope. "I want all my kids and grandkids to have encounters with God that they never recover from. I want them to see dreams and visions. I want them to be knocked off their horse of selfishness to rely on the Lord. I want my kids to have heavenly encounters."

So, I spoke and wrote these declarations. "I want to be so blessed financially that God will be able to do anything, everything through me He wants." And God gave me some great verses on that theme to declare. Are you listening? I want to walk in divine health. And I wrote two reasons for walking in divine health: to glorify God and to provoke people to want to know the secret of such healthy living so they would want to know God. Again, the Lord gave me so many promises on divine health.

Also, I wrote this hope: "I want a greater hunger for the Word of God, because everything I want is in the Word. I am hoping for a greater hunger for the Word." Are we hungry for more of the Word?

Then, I wrote: "I want deeper revelation in the Word and the Holy Spirit. I want to excel in the Word and the Spirit." The previous night I had a vision, a dream about salvation as a meal. I want you to envision this right now with me. Imagine an apple the size of our neighborhood. Let's call it salvation, the nature of God, the meal that never ends, the banquet table. Most people take a bite to be forgiven or a bite for hope when they're in trouble. But let's imagine feasting on a huge apple the size of our neighborhood, full of joy for us to eat. God is waiting on us to begin.

So, one of my hopes: "I want a greater revelation that comes from a greater hunger. I want so much revelation in the Word and the Spirit that I cannot discern where I end and where He begins. I want to disappear so that Jesus has so much joy living through me!"

Are you thinking I'm wacky now? Well, there's more! "I also hope and want to declare God's Word over my life daily. I don't want to miss one day." I've been doing this three or four times each day. When thoughts come to mind, I start speaking out loud what am I hoping for. I declare words of faith and hope over my life, my family, my friends, my ministry, my partners, my Zoom family. Whatever hope comes to my mind, I refuse to leave it in the realm of thoughts. I want it to release seeds!

This is what I'm trying to communicate: Faith needs to be active. Faith by itself is useless without words. And faith is released through His Word in my words. So, every time you desire something, speak to promise, speak to provision, speak to miracle! Anytime hope comes alive, speak it out!

Here is one more hope I share with you: I want to be a doer of the word, not just a hearer. I want the Word to become flesh. I want everything the Word says to be reality in my life. I want to be a doer of the Word." Do you want to be a doer of the Word?

Those were the first things I wrote down. I won't give you the others, but these will give you an idea of how the Spirit is teaching me to apply faith, practice faith, activate faith.

## NOW FAITH!

I start declaring the Word. I start declaring it over my family, my kids, my grandkids, and every situation I face every day. For example, I'm declaring daily that all the villages where our ministry wants to drill wells in Africa, Pakistan, and anywhere else will receive safe water.

But that is not enough! We want every village with safe water to walk in faith, to be born again into Jesus, filled with the Spirit, discipled in the Word, and gathered to worship in congregations. If the Lord, our team, and our partners can drill 14 wells, we can lead and disciple 1400 people into Jesus, and start 140 congregations. Then, the Lord can help us drill hundreds of wells, lead and disciple thousands with faith in Christ, and start hundreds of congregations.

Everything has to start with a seed. That's what the Kingdom is like. That's the verse we started with: "The kingdom of God is like a person sowing seed in soil." Amen!

# 4

# REIGNING IN OUR HEARTS ALREADY

Together, we are learning lessons from the Lord and the Word about the transformative power of faith. When we realize and activate words of faith in the power of the Spirit, we can renew generations, congregations, denominations, and nations. We are what we say. We reflect and resemble what we say. We influence others by our words, for better or worse. The LORD God is the most powerful force in the universe and words are some of the most dynamic and influential forces on Earth.

Let's lay the foundation in Genesis 1:1 where Moses wrote, "In the beginning, God created the heavens and the earth. The earth was a formless and desolate emptiness. Darkness was over the surface of the deep. The Spirit of God was hovering over the surface of the waters." Notice Scripture doesn't record that 80% of God's Spirit was hovering or 90% of God was there. The Word insists that the entirety of the Spirit of God was hovering over the waters at the creation of the whole world.

God's Spirit is always present. Listen carefully: God's Spirit is always present when He is getting ready to release His Word. This is a very important truth. God's Spirit is always present. On the dark, flip side, the spirit of satan is also present when God is getting ready to release His Word.

Then God said, "Let there be light." Remember, God always says what He desires. In Genesis 1:26-28 God created by speaking, "Let us make mankind in our image, according to our likeness. And let them rule over the fish of the sea, over the birds of the sky, over the livestock, over all the earth, and over every crawling thing that crawls on the earth. So, God created man, in His own image, in the image of God, He created him. Male and female He created them. God blessed them. And God said to them, 'Be fruitful and multiply. Fill the earth and subdue it. Have dominion over the fish of the sea, the birds of the sky, and everything that moves on the earth.'" So, God gave humanity authority to rule the earth.

A few verses earlier in Genesis 1:11 the LORD also declared, "Let the earth sprout vegetation: plants yielding seed and fruit trees on the earth, bearing fruit according to their kind with seed in them.' And it was so." Everything God created, He created with words. And everything He created with words, have the seed in themselves to reproduce after their own kind. God's words were the seeds that produced all things that have seeds. This is why it's important to make sure we're saying what we want, and not saying what we don't want.

In agreement, Proverbs 4:24 instructs, "Rid yourself of a deceitful mouth. Keep devious speech far from you." What is a deceitful mouth? It is a mouth that speaks things contrary to God's desire. What is God's desire? His Word. So, if we're speaking things that don't agree with God's Word, we're speaking with devious or perverse lips. This would be like saying, "I'll always be sick. I will never be healed. I'll never get a breakthrough. I will always be depressed. I'll always be poor. My business will never grow. My ministry is never going to flourish. Revival will never come to my city." This is a litany of perverse speech narratives. And none of these doubting, fearful words come from the Word of God. None of them proclaim faith.

# NOW FAITH!

Do you sincerely believe the Bible is God's will for us? Do you believe God's Word is His will for mankind? Great. God's words are His will for mankind. But even though we're created in the image of God, when we do not believe He has authority to rule this world, then our words will reflect what our own will is for our life. A lot of times, we make statements in jest, sarcasm, or cynicism. We randomly speak some things that God does not desire and even what we do not desire. Our negative, doubting, unbelieving words still have a lot of power.

Proverbs 18:21 reminds us that the power of life and death is in our tongue. Please say this aloud: The power of life and death is in my tongue. So, we can say things that bring life. And we can say things that bring death. God gave us authority to rule this planet with words that we declare with our mouths. And our words release either the power of God or the power of satan. Are you getting this? So, words conceived in our spirit produce words in our mouth. Then, our words produce what we willfully decide to declare. Our words that come out of our mouth have capacity to conceive, to reproduce the powerful seed of our actual words.

Listen to this: our words either release the power of God or the power of satan. People have said to me so many times, "Well, this doesn't work. My kids are all lost. I don't have any money. I'm sick. This is the worst year of my life." Then, I look at them quietly. Do you know what I tell them? "It's working perfectly. You are living exactly what you're saying." But many times, they don't see it: the light doesn't come on and they persist in speaking unbelief.

Our words release either the authority of God's presence or the power of satan's presence. God's presence gives life. Satan's presence brings death. Both of those outcomes hinge on what we say. Faith comes by hearing God (Romans 10:17). Fear comes by hearing Satan. What are we hearing the most? Come on. We hear most what we are saying. We are hearing ourselves the most. So, if we're speaking what

God says, faith is flowing and growing. But if we're speaking what satan says, fear is growing and faith is decreasing, even disappearing. Faith comes from hearing God's words. Fear comes from hearing satan's words.

Philippians 4:13 is an amazing verse on this theme: "I can do all things through Christ who strengthens me." In what good way could that verse become reality in our life? By practicing Joshua 1:8, "Don't let this book of the law depart from your mouth. But be careful to meditate on it day and night, never letting it depart from you. Be careful to do all that is written therein. Your way will be made prosperous and everything you put your hands to will be successful." That verse means always let God's Word be what we're saying. We must never quit, delay, or avoid speaking God's Word: in our praying, in our marriage, in our family, in our conversing, in our rest, in our driving, in our studying, and in our working. If we are not feeling what the Word is saying, we should speak words opposite of what we're feeling.

I experienced one of the most amazing weekends of my life in Fort Worth, Texas with Pastor Dr. C. B. Glidden. On Sunday morning, as he introduced me for the final service, he became emotional with tears streaming down his face. He said, "You know, I have never seen anything like what God is doing here. I really didn't even know this was possible." At age 60, he's been pastoring his whole life. That morning, all of us present saw so much power he released into people through his words of faith. That morning, the Spirit produced much fruit that remains!

However, that night, when I got back to my hotel room, I could barely walk because of my own pain. I had to make a choice. Was I going to speak words of fear, discouragement, readiness to quit, and hopelessness? Or was I going to say opposite of what I was feeling in the natural? I had a choice to make. So, I started commanding pain to leave. I started receiving the sacrifice of the blood of Jesus. I started speaking the truth of the Word. And the more I spoke the Word and declared faith in the LORD, the better I felt.

Why does speaking God's Word release God's power in our life? That's an interesting question. Why does speaking God's Word release God's power in our life? God's Word is His nature. We have no right or reason to separate God's Word from His Personhood. His Word is the DNA of His nature. God's Word is His bond, His character, and His essence.

According to Psalm 138:2, "God magnifies His Word as high as His name." According to John 1:1, "In the beginning was the Word." Right? God's Word represents Himself in Person. So, when we speak God's word, we receive Him and release His power into our life. When we release the written Word with our voice, His Word in our voice leads us to the Living Word, Jesus the Messiah. His Word is the spiritual DNA, the essence of God. So, when we speak His Word, we hear it in our inner ear.

I challenge you to do something that might make you feel a little uncomfortable. Record your voice on an answering machine, phone, or another device. Then, listen to yourself. You will hear yourself the way others hear you. They are hearing you with their outer ear. When I review a recording of my teaching, it sounds like somebody else talking. Why? Because I am accustomed to hearing myself with my inner ear, which is my heart and my spirit.

Now, here's an interesting scientific, biological discovery. The part of the brain that affects speech is connected to every nerve in your body. There are 100,000 connection points to every nerve in our body that come from that part in the brain that controls speech.

Remember, God made us in His image. How did the Lord use His speech? Here are a few examples. When God saw darkness, He spoke light. When Jesus saw storms, He spoke peace. God always uses words to overcome contradictions to His will. All of us have been created in the image of God with the ability to declare his Word and to overcome contradictions to His will.

We're all born in sin and contradiction to God's will. You know my story and I know some of your stories. So, we have a choice. Do we agree to contradict the will of God and speak the will of satan? Or will we keep speaking the will of God by declaring his Word over our life? That's our choice. No one can force us to do either of these. Nobody can sow our seed for us. Each of us is the only one who can sow our own seed.

Let's review ways God gave us ability to use words to overcome contradictions to His will, which should be our will. If we are trying to follow Christ, we should want in our lives only what Christ wants in our lives. In Mark 9:23, Jesus looked at a doubting man and said, "If you can? All things are possible to the one who believes." Well, if faith comes by hearing, then what could help us believe? That's right: saying what God's Word says. "All things are possible to the one who believes." And belief is the byproduct of faith and faith comes by hearing. If we really want to receive all things, we need to say what God's Word says so His will becomes what we believe. Amen?

In Matthew 21:22, Jesus promised, "Whatever you ask in prayer believing, you will receive it all." Jesus believed, practiced, and taught that. And He cannot lie. Again, Jesus said in Mark 9:23, "All things are possible to the one who believes." If you've had a disease for 50 years, would that be included in all things? Come on!

Let's look at Mark 11:23 where Jesus said, "Whoever says to this mountain 'Be taken up and thrown into the sea,' and does not doubt in his heart but believes that he says is going to happen, it will be granted to him." Do we believe what He says? Continue: "Therefore I say to you, all things for which you pray and believe, ask and believe that you have received them, and they will be granted to you." Jesus said that whatever we pray, if we believe it, we will receive it.

Now, let's gaze at Jesus. For a minute, don't look at your Bible or this book. Look at Jesus for a minute. With faith. In His Word. Gaze longer than a glance. He is eager for us to hear Him now as His Spirit speaks to us. What does He say? What do you want to say to Him?

Please read this carefully. We're never going to believe what we're saying or what we're praying unless we know it's God's will. I repeat: to believe what we're saying or praying is not possible unless we know that is God's will. And what is God's will? His will is His Word. Do we get it and believe it? Do we know His Word? If we're saying what is in the Word, then we can actually believe it. And if we actually believe it, we will receive it.

In John 5:19 we find the secret of Jesus' success in His ministry. "Jesus answered and was saying to them, 'Truly, truly I say to you, the Son can do nothing of himself unless it is something He sees the Father doing. For whatever the Father does, these things the Son also does in the same way.'" Jesus would not do one thing unless He saw His Father doing that.

Now, let's receive Jesus' words in John 12:49, "I did not speak on my own, but the Father Himself who sent Me has given Me a commandment as to what to say and what to speak." So, Jesus would never do one thing unless He saw the Father doing that. And Jesus would never say anything unless He heard the Father saying that.

What could happen if that is all we did and all we said? Seriously, let's think about that. Remember, I challenged us to confess over ourselves every day what the Word of God says over us. Right? What if all we said was what God is saying over our lives, our marriages, our kids, our congregation, our work, and over everything? What if all we did was to release God's Word? We'll never know without trying, will we?

In Psalm 45:1 we read, "Your tongue is the pen of a ready writer." The LORD wants us to speak words that we want Him to write on our heart. And here is Proverbs 3:1-3 paraphrased, "He wants His Word written on our hearts, engraved on our hearts, because we speak what is on our heart." Also, in Proverbs 4:20, "My son (or daughter), pay attention to my words. Incline your ear to my sayings. They are not to escape from your sight." Here we have a capsulation of faith. That is, faith comes by hearing and faith is made perfect by seeing. Think about that. The writer of Proverbs is instructing us with wisdom: don't stop listening and don't stop seeing. These are primary sources of faith in Jesus.

Paul wrote in Romans 10:17, "Faith is made perfect by seeing." Again, Proverbs 4:20 teaches, "Incline your ear to my sayings. They are not to escape from your sight. Keep them in your heart." Keep planting the Word of God in your heart, in your soil, in your spirit, in your field where you want a harvest. Keep putting My words in your heart for they are life to those who find them, and healing to all their body." Will we embrace that? Come on!

I noted in my 2022 journal that I felt flu-type symptoms come on me five times across the year: sinus problem, a sore throat, a little nausea, and similar issues. Each time, I rebuked it with the Word of God, and most of it left within a couple of hours. One held on the longest, almost a day and a half, but I never got sick. Because I kept the Word before my eyes, I kept the Word in my mouth. This is not something someone can do for us. No one else can sow our seeds! We need to think and speak words of faith for those seeds to become health to all our body. I didn't get sick for almost two years. Everybody around me got sick. Church: what are we saying? Are we thinking in our heart and speaking what Satan is saying? Are we saying what the culture is saying, what the world is saying? Or are we speaking what God is saying?

I saw that somebody posted about one of the episodes of "The Chosen". I was sad. In that scene, a disciple came to Jesus and said, "I'm sick." And in the episode Jesus said, "I'm sorry. I'm not going to heal you, because the Father wants to teach you through your sickness." This grieved me, because that is part of a religious system that will be all over the planet before Jesus comes back.

Not only will the political system make faith hard. The religious system will also buy into a form of godliness but will deny the power. No one should make up conversations about Jesus that are not in the Word of God. Nowhere in Scripture did someone come to Jesus for healing, and He responded, "No." That's not in the Scripture. Satan is going to be that subtle, even in a popular series like "The Chosen" when everybody is emotional and loves the story line.

Some will begin to recall this little scene when anyone looking for an excuse not to believe in healing will begin to think that Jesus doesn't always heal. They become further influenced by a series well-produced, but that does not accurately portray what the Word of God says about the life and power of Jesus. That's how subtle it is. And then people say, "Well see, I told you." Jesus cannot return until His Bride is doing what He did. We cannot look at people with hard cases and say, "No, God wants to teach you through your hard case."

We need to look at people who are diseased or born blind, like the man in John 9. When the disciples were looking for a reason for blindness and asked Jesus, "Who sinned?" Remember Jesus responded, "This isn't sin. This happened so that every time a believer faces an impossible situation such as blindness, the works of God might be displayed with prayers of faith and authority of the Word. Not every time we face a contradiction to the Word of God is a time to look for the cause of the problem. Instead, we have an opportunity to release the power of the Kingdom. Amen?

When Satan came against Jesus with temptation in the wilderness, how did Jesus respond? With the Word of God. Jesus always responded with the Word of His Father. His power was the Word to overcome satan. If we're ever going to receive faith from God's Word, we need to have faith in God's Word. Please repeat now aloud with personal commitment: If we're ever going to receive faith from God's Word, we need to have faith in God's Word.

Some of us are facing stress or some form of distress right now. So, we need to receive and declare Hebrews 11:1, "Faith is the substance of things hoped for, and the evidence of things not seen." The substance of our faith is what we're desiring. But the substance of fear is what we don't want. Our faith comes by saying what we want, based on God's Word. Our fear comes by saying what we don't want, based on symptoms or circumstances that satan will use to distract and deceive.

This brings us to James 1:26, "A person who claims to have religion, but has not yet learned to bridle his tongue, deceives himself." Do we perceive this problem? Sometimes we are in a tight fix, or we don't feel good, or we feel lonely, or we feel depressed, or we feel pressure, or we feel fear. Then suddenly, we speak those troubled feelings flow out in matching words. God designed our heart to produce what we say. Our heart believes that what we say is what we want. That's why we study the parable of the sower in Mark 4:26, "The kingdom of God is like a man who sows seeds. How it works he doesn't know. But he goes to bed, and he wakes up and the soil automatically produces the seed." The seed is our heart.

Our heart thinks that whatever we say is what we want. Some say, "I'm afraid. I'm just going to stay sick. I'm not going to be healed. I am going to die with this." If we speak words such as these, our heart believes them and responds, "How will I make that work? It seems that is what he or she wants." Then, we fellowship or worship with believers and we speak opposite words such as, "Oh, we believe in healing. We believe in revival. We believe in peace. We believe we can be set free." So, now our heart is hearing that clear contrast, and our heart becomes deceived. Our heart is disturbed and wonders, "In one moment: death. In the next moment: trying to release revival. So, which does this person want?"

Our heart is deceived because we haven't learned to bridle our tongue. We really don't believe that one of the most powerful forces in the world is our words. What we say is what our heart thinks we want. So, we need to be careful to say only what we want. Do we really hear this? We need to be careful to only say what we want.

In Mark 4:14, the sower sows the Word. You and I are the ones sowing the Word. Nobody else is sowing it for us. Every word we speak is a seed. I will illustrate from my family again and expand on a few thoughts I wrote in the first chapter. My mom and dad are older than 90. My mama has only and always spoken positive words. My daddy is more prone to speaking negative words. Can you guess who is happier? Mama. Can you guess who people think about when they say, "When we are with this woman, we feel like we have been with Jesus?" Mama. Why? Because her whole life she has only sown seeds of faith, hope, love, and peace.

I was talking with her not long ago. Family members were saying that Mama might not live long because her health is failing. Well, she looked at me and said, "You know, I'm going live to 110." And I asked her, "How do you know that?" She responded, "Because there are far too many people who still need my love and prayer for me to leave already." That's the only reason she wants to stay alive. How is this possible? It's impossible to defeat a person like her. All she has sown her whole life is faith, hope, love, and peace.

In my whole life, I have never heard my mom say a negative thing: never. Never! Around my daddy, we need to be careful which day we talk with him. Because he is a byproduct of his words. I can visit their home, talk face to face with him, and share recent Bible discoveries for 10-minutes. He will start crying and will be encouraged for six hours. Then, someone will say something, and he falls right back into a dungeon emotionally and verbally. What is the point? Our words are one of the most powerful forces in the world.

To illustrate further from the Word in Joshua 1:8, "Don't let this book of the law depart from your mouth but be careful to meditate on it day and night." The word "meditate" means "to murmur, talk to yourself, or chew on it." The analogy I think of again is a cow that chews a cud. A cow chews, chews, and chews until the cud leaves the first stomach and goes into the second stomach. Then, the cow chews, chews, and chews until the cud leaves the second stomach into the third stomach. After chewing more, the cud leaves the third stomach into the fourth stomach. And it keeps chewing until somehow, out of grass, that cud becomes 1000 pounds of steak. How? It chews on something.

That's a picture of what the Word could produce in us. Not 1,000 pounds of flesh, but the manifestation of everything that is in the Word. I haven't mastered this in private all the time yet. I have a slight advantage because I get to study, meditate on, and proclaim the Word. So, when I'm sharing my heart with you, the Lord is also encouraging and developing me. I am blessed to practice in public with amazing people such as you what I want to be 24/7 in private.

Jesus fulfilled this 24/7 in private and in public. Jesus always said only what His Father told Him to say. And He promised we can become just like Him. Does anybody think we have room to grow in declaring words of faith?

Before we conclude, let's receive further insight into Jesus from Mark 4:26. Jesus was saying, "The kingdom of God is like a man who cast seeds upon the soil." If you want to know what it looks like to live the kingdom of God, it's like somebody who never stops believing and speaking the Word of God. God's Word is the seed. We never stop sowing the Word.

Again, I illustrate. Recently, I was eating dinner in a restaurant before I preached that evening. After dinner, when the waitress came to clear the table, I could discern she wasn't a believer. The Lord said to me, "Give her a cash tip to bless her. That gift will open her heart so you can pray for her." By the Holy Spirit I knew in my spirit she was repulsed by Christianity. But few I know are repulsed by a gift of money. Do you hear this?

So, I looked at her and said, "You're the best waitress I've ever had." She responded, "Really?"

I said, "Yes, and I want you to receive this. I already added a tip to the check, but I want to give you this cash to double your tip." She asked, "Why?"

Ready in my spirit, I replied, "Because I want to pray for you." She backed up a little and said, "Oh, I think I'm okay."

Still ready for her response, I said, "I know. I know you're okay. But I want to pray that this tip would become normal for you, and you'll be so overcome with blessing, you won't know what happened. Then, you'll remember this prayer. So, can I pray for you?" She looked at me and said, "I guess."

So, I put my hand on her shoulder and prayed that she would receive more blessing until she wouldn't know how to respond. She would know that some caring man released a prayer that changed the course of her life.

After I finished praying briefly, she looked at me strangely, smiled a little, and said, "Thank you. Thank you." Now, here is what she didn't know: Jesus lives inside of me. I believe I am His hands. I'm his body. I touched her shoulder, which means the DNA of Jesus got on her. I released His Word, which means there are seeds in her heart whether she knows it or not and whether she likes it or not.

There was a possibility that days or weeks from that encounter with Jesus in me, she would wake up at 3:00 in the morning and imagine a picture of what Jesus did in a word-of-faith seed-exchange. That is what the Kingdom is like. "It's like a person who goes around and sows seed." Do you hear this?

Sometimes we get to see a miracle. Sometimes we get to see salvation. Sometimes we merely see the seed being sown. Jesus was saying, "The kingdom of God is like a man who casts seed upon the soil. He goes to bed at night, and he gets up daily. The seed sprouts and grows, but he doesn't have a clue how it happens." The soil produces crops all by itself. When we get seed in our heart, our heart will produce it. When we get seed in our heart, our heart will produce it all by itself. "First the stalk, then the head, then the mature grain. When the crop permits, immediately you can put your sickle out, because the harvest has come."

So, where is this Kingdom? Jesus said in Luke 17:20-21, "The Kingdom is in you. The Kingdom of God is in you." The King reigns in our heart. The Kingdom of God that produces everything the Word of God says is in our heart. It is in our heart, waiting to receive a seed. Then, it can produce what's already in the soil. Please read this aloud: "The

# NOW FAITH!

Kingdom of God is already in my heart, waiting for me to plant a seed that releases everything that is already in me. Automatically!"

Do we need healing? Let's plant a seed for healing in our body. It's already in our heart. Because in the Kingdom, everyone is already healed. "By His stripes you were healed." Come on! Faith seeds for healing are already in our heart, not only in our body. Everything that is in heaven is in us, waiting to come alive with a seed that we are willing to speak.

Now, let's apply Philippians 4:19, "My God will supply all of your needs, according to..." how bad you're doing? Oh, the Word doesn't say that. it says, "...according to His glorious riches in Christ Jesus." Our needs are supplied by Christ. And He is the Word of God.

Let's find a way to highlight these next words. As food is for the stomach and seed is for the soil, words are for the heart. Again, speak these words slowly and thoughtfully for your ear to hear: As food is for the stomach and seed is for the soil, words are for the heart. So, God's Word, words that come from Him, produce life and power. On the contrary, words that come from satan produce fear, doubt, and unbelief.

Romans 10:8 reminds each of us, "The word is near you, in your mouth and in your heart. That is the word of faith, which we are preaching: that if you confess with your mouth that Jesus is Lord and believe in your heart that God raised Him from the dead, you will be saved." Isn't that amazing?

One Sunday morning when I finished preaching, I wanted to pray for people to receive the baptism in the Holy Spirit, but I reminded them they needed to be in the family of God first. In other words, we need to be born of the Spirit so we can be baptized in the Spirit.

I sat at the front very quietly and asked, "Does anyone want to be born again today and receive Jesus Christ as your Savior so you can be the body of Christ?" And one by one, 13 people walked up to the front of that sanctuary. And every time somebody walked up, the congregation were cheering, shouting, and clapping. I didn't know whether all of them needed to be born again. I'm not the judge of that. But one by one, they walked to the front, visible to hundreds of people.

Then, I led them in a simple prayer so they would say aloud what the Word says is reality. I said, "Believe what I pray and then repeat it out loud after me." After they and I prayed, I encouraged them by saying, "You're saved, born again." Isn't this amazing! Romans 10:10 assures us, "With the heart a person believes." So, when we believe the Word, the result is righteousness, the nature of God. When we believe, we are the righteousness of God. "With the mouth, he confesses, resulting in salvation."

What is salvation? Forgiveness, deliverance, healing, protection, guidance, prosperity, and wholeness in Christ Jesus. When we believe, all this in our heart is waiting for us to say it. Then, we can experience it. When we believe, all the supernatural hope, love, joy, and peace in our heart is waiting for us to say it. Then, we can start experiencing it.

Again, what does the Lord and the Word say in Romans 10:8? We always start with what does the Lord say? What does the Word say? "The Word is near you. It is in your mouth, so you can put it in your heart." Amen! Do you see this? When we speak the Word of God with our mouth, we can receive it in our heart.

Faith comes by hearing and speaking the Word. We need to live in the Word and speak the Word until the Word that is written comes alive in us. This is what we read in 2 Corinthians 4:13, "Since we have the same spirit of faith, according to what is written, "I believed, therefore I spoke." We believe, therefore we also speak. This could become contagious. If we start saying what we believe, then other people might catch on and start saying what they believe. Then, suddenly, our congregations could celebrate a bunch of believers saying what they believe, instead of saying what they fear.

So, the more we speak the Word, the more we believe it. And the more we believe it, the more we speak it. And the more we speak it, the more we believe it. And the more we believe it, the more we speak it. And the more we speak it, the more we believe it. Then, what we are believing and speaking, speaking and believing, that becomes our nature. And Matthew 12:34 becomes our reality: "We're now speaking out of the overflow of our heart." We have so much good seed in the soil of our heart that we speak only what is coming out of the Word overflowing from our heart.

A harvest of faith does not depend on God alone. A harvest of faith also depends on seeds we are willing to plant and to speak from our heart. God is not going to plant our seeds. He's not going to force feed us the seed. He's not going to open a portal in heaven and inject us with seed through a long syringe from heaven. The Lord is waiting for us to use our authority to release His power through our words. He's waiting on us to plant what we want to receive.

So, here's the question. Are we planting bad weeds? Or good seeds? They will both grow. And here's the problem. The weeds grow a lot easier. Things that are not in the Word usually spring up easier than the things that are in the Word. So here are some things we should never say. Are we ready for this? We should never say, "Well, God knows what I need." That's a dumb statement. Obviously, He does. And we still need it because He is waiting on us to do something about it. We should never say, "Well, God knows what I need."

Or how about this? We should never say, "Well, I just don't understand the Bible." That's like me saying, "I just don't understand calculus." Then, you know what? I never will. Do you know why? I'm not going to study it. Ever. Is that a helpful analogy? I know, you calculus buffs are saying, "Wait a minute, it's easy." Well, maybe it is for you because you studied it. Do you know what is easy for me? The Word. Why? I stay in the Word and don't get out of it. Like I'm standing in quicksand Word. I can't get out of it. I'm in this big pool of the Word. I'm a prisoner of hope. I'm in a life sentence of hope with no chance of parole.

We should never say, "I'll never be healed. I'll never get ahead financially. My family will never be functional. My ministry can never flourish. Let's decide to never speak words that go against the Word. Let's say only what God's Word says!

If we can't say it aloud, whisper it. We watch what we plant. We don't say, "Well, it's influenza season." That's a seed, friend. "Well, another cold is coming around." That's a seed. "Well, you know, it's that time of the month." That's a seed. "When the weather changes, my joints hurt." That's a seed.

Why don't we stop planting weeds? Why don't we start planting seeds? Seeds that produce the Kingdom? Amen?

I close with this. Not long ago, I received an email from a lady who is experiencing debilitating pain. While lying on a bed of affliction, she has participated in our team Zoom calls frequently. Her name is Karen. For 23 years, she was a physical therapist. Ten years ago, she was given an injection, an epidural that produced adverse effects in her nerves, muscles, and all her tissues. Now, she's bedfast. She cannot move and is in constant pain. But she is wrestling the good fight of faith, standing on the Word of God. Most people left her alone because they said she didn't have enough faith. So, I'm not

# NOW FAITH!

saying that if you'll do this, everything happens automatically. I'm not saying that. I am not naive.

I'm teaching faith because it's what God's Word teaches. Jesus said, "All things are possible to the one who believes." Now that might offend us. That might make us feel badly or that might hurt our feelings. I am simply trying to reiterate what Jesus said. The Son of God said, "Whatsoever things you ask in prayer, believing, you'll receive it all." Jesus said that. So, I'm trying to teach faith at least 100 different ways. If we want our prayers and our words to be in belief, then "faith comes by hearing the Word." Faith doesn't come any other way. If you say, "Well, I'll believe it when I see it." Then, we'll always be susceptible to circumstances in our flesh. If we persist in unbelief, we'll be carnal; we'll never be spiritual.

Then, we never will believe because we will only be as good as our last breakthrough. The reason why I'm pressing these principles of faith is because this is the way Jesus taught faith. And it goes against everything that's natural or carnal or the way that seems right to people, and that way gets broader and wider. Jesus' way gets narrower and narrower, because the end result of living the faith should be Psalm 91 where we learn that no evil could come near us, nothing could touch us.

I'm not trying to offend anybody. I'm sorry if people are offended by the truth of the Word. When Jesus comes back to earth, I don't want to be one of the persons He asks, "Will I even find faith?" I want to be one of the persons about whom Jesus says, "Those persons believe. They never stop believing. Nothing can happen that causes them to stop believing. They just keep believing." So, the Lord called me to raise up an army of believers with authentic, enduring faith. Jesus said in John 11:40, "Did I not tell you that if you believe, you would see the glory of God?" Friends, I want to see the glory of God. Amen?

# 5

# LIVING BY FAITH, NOT BY FLESH

One Sunday morning where I was preaching, six people helped lead worship ministry, so I took them to lunch afterwards. One of the ladies in the group said, "Dan, you provoked me."

I asked, "Was that a good provoke or a bad provoke?" She affirmed, "Since I met you, I love to listen to the Bible all the time. I am eager to study the Bible all the time. I am compelled to dig into the Bible all the time. As I apply it to my life, the Word has changed me. I'm provoked by your teaching more faith in Jesus." I responded, "Good. Then I want to keep provoking you."

In Luke 18:8, the Lord Jesus Christ asked His disciples, "When the Son of Man comes the second time, will He find faith on the earth?" We desire to be some of those people in whom He will find faith! We believe in Him the Living Word and in the Bible, the written Word.

We are living by faith, not by the flesh, not by sight, and not by what is evident through our five senses. We live by what we can read and validate from the infallible Word. The Word cannot lie. We are attempting to scale the heights of faith, and dig the depths of faith, and to be provoked by faith.

Here is another recent testimony of faith in the Word from one of my "home churches" in LaCygne, Kansas. A young lady who came with her daddy told me what the Lord had done two years previously when I went there the first time. She said, "You might not know how God used you to change my family and me. My daddy had been addicted to nicotine his whole life and couldn't quit smoking. You laid hands on my daddy. Now, he has never touched a cigarette for two years. He has not had one desire for a cigarette in two years."

She continued, "You also prayed for me because I was depressed and suicidal. Now, I haven't been sad or depressed one minute since that day in that service. There's more. Two of my relatives have been in lethal car wrecks, and there is no way they should be alive. I was able to lay my hands on them by faith. Now, they're both fine."

More recently, she talked with me again, "Dan, I have been practicing what you teach on your Bible studies through Zoom. I had a friend who had a deadly sickness, so I laid hands on her and prayed. One week later, she was fine."

This young lady could not stop talking about the power of the Holy Spirit, and what the Holy Spirit can do. So, I want to encourage us to stay in the faith. Let's remain strong in the faith! If we live in the faith, "all things are possible to the one who believes." Amen? Do we really believe that? "All things are possible to the one who believes" (Mark 9:23).

I want to teach again about how faith works. "Faith comes by hearing," so we need to hear it. Somebody needs to declare it. And why wouldn't we declare faith by hearing if we're the some of the persons who need to hear it?

Let's explore Luke 1:26 and following verses. I want to explore a conversation that Mary had with the angel of the Lord. "Now, in the

# NOW FAITH!

sixth month, the angel Gabriel was sent from God to a city in Galilee named Nazareth, to a virgin betrothed to a man whose name was Joseph, of the descendants of David. And the virgin's name was Mary. Coming in, he said to her, 'Greetings, favored one, the Lord is with you.

"Now, she was perplexed at this statement, and was pondering what kind of greeting this was." Let's pause there a moment. I remind us: whether we feel it or not, the Lord is with us. Now, let's think about the possibilities of that. The creator of the universe is inside us right now. The Redeemer of the entire, global human race, lives inside our spirit. Do you comprehend the gravity of this? God is in us!

"She was perplexed about what kind of greeting this was. And then the angel said to her, 'Do not be afraid, Mary, you have found favor with God. And behold, you will conceive in your womb and give birth to a son. And you shall name him Jesus.'"

That is a stunning conversation! First, God is with you! Next, you have found favor. Finally, you're pregnant. This is a shocking revelation. But there's more! "And He will be great and be called the Son of the Most High. The LORD God will give Him the throne of His father, David. And He will reign over the house of Jacob forever, and His kingdom will have no end.' But Mary said to the angel, 'How will this be since I am a virgin?'"

Let's pause there and think about this for a little bit. Ladies, you know it's impossible to get pregnant in your womb if you're a virgin. You can have thoughts in your mind about becoming pregnant. In your heart and emotions, you can imagine getting pregnant. But Gabriel specifically said to Mary: "You will conceive in your womb," So, Mary, this pregnancy will be in your flesh, not merely in your mind or emotions.

This would be a good time to ask a question, wouldn't it? If something is not humanly possible, it's okay to ask a question. I remind people everywhere I minister that it's okay to ask questions if we don't understand how it's possible. However, it's not okay to question God's Word. In other words, it's okay to ask the question, "How can you do this?" But we should never question the integrity or character of God. Because if He says it, He can do it.

Some people have situations in families, kids not walking with Jesus, business problems, ministry challenges, financial disasters, or physical conditions. Maybe there are a thousand problems. But I guarantee every person reading this book, every one of our family members, everyone in our congregations, and all of colleagues at work face some kind of problem.

Imagine how we would respond if God said to us right now, "Don't worry, I will handle that problem." Our response would likely be, "How is this possible?" I repeat: it's okay to ask God, "How is this possible?" Do we want Him to answer it? Come on! He is the answer! Our faith often pauses to ask our questions, but the Word of God is always the answer for whatever question we ask. God's Word is the answer that stops the question mark from stopping our faith. Aren't you glad? Don't you love the Word of God?

For example, we might ask, "Lord, how in the world can I ever get ahead financially?" His answer: "Give and it shall be given to you, pressed down, shaken together, and running over." People will give into our genuine need. Come on!

If we sow good seed when we don't know how it's possible in the year of famine, God could give us a 100-fold return! God's Word always has an answer to our questions.

For example, we might say, "I wonder if I can be healed." Wait a minute! God promises, "I sent my Word and healed you. Those who

# NOW FAITH!

find my Word find life and health for all their body. By my stripes, you were already healed." God's Word always answers our questions. So, we ask the Lord and search the Word with our questions.

This is a revelation we want each person to receive. We should not ask the world our questions. Instead, let's ask the Word our questions! Let's quit asking the world our questions. Get off of Google. Get in the Bible. Are you hearing and receiving this revelation?

Here is our problem: we go to the world for our answers. That merely leads to more questions. Instead, we need to go to the Lord Jesus and the Word of God for our answers. And the Lord of the Word will lead us to the solution. Amen? If we really are believing followers and learners, we would be giving each other "high fives". Wouldn't we? Shouldn't we?

Back to Mary who asked, "'How is this possible since I'm a virgin?' The angel answered and said to her, 'The Holy Spirit will come upon you and the power of the Most High will overshadow you. For that reason, the Holy Child will be called the Son of God. And behold, even your relative Elizabeth herself has conceived a son in her old age. And she who was once called infertile, is now in her sixth month.'"

Isn't it amazing how often God gives us a testimony through someone else's life, a testimony similar to what we need in our own life? God knows how to dispense testimonies in someone else's circumstance that we're dealing with in our circumstance! Come on! We ought to be happy that He is willing, ready, and able to say, "I know you're having a hard time being pregnant in this relationship because you're a virgin, but your relative Elizabeth who is too old to have kids is six months pregnant also." So, nothing is impossible when God says something unusual will happen. Nothing is impossible!

Some time ago, while I was ministering in Texas, I was speaking words of knowledge in the Holy Spirit, and a man's hip was healed.

Well, that night after the service at about 11 o'clock, I was in bed in extreme pain. For some reason, my hip was extraordinarily painful. And I didn't know how I was going to get to the restroom because it hurt too much to even try to walk. At that precise moment, I received a text from the pastor with the testimony of a lady whose hip was healed while watching the service on livestream.

She had not been able to walk and stand straight without pain for several years. As soon as I read that testimony, faith entered my spirit and soul, and the Lord strengthened my hip. I got up and I was able to walk across the room, because God knows when we need a testimony! When He has worked in someone else's life, He is able to give faith for the same healing we're needing Him to work in our lives. I want you to know that is how good our Papa, our Abba is. Isn't that good news?

We read more Good News in Luke: "For nothing will be impossible with God." That's one of the most profound verses in the whole Bible. No thing! The word "thing" there is the Greek word Rhema. Every spoken word of God can accomplish what He intends. Anything God says is possible. Nothing God says is impossible.

Then, Mary's response to the Lord's Rhema was, "'Behold, the Lord's bond servant. May this be done to me, according to your Word.' And the angel departed from her." I don't know how much time elapsed between her faith agreement with God's Word and her reality in pregnancy. I think it was instantaneous. I think God waited 4,000 years for a virgin to agree with His Word, and let it become a reality. And when she spoke, "May this be done," the faith seed of her word allowed the Word to become flesh. Then, nine months later, He was born and dwelt among us. This is profound to me!

God didn't force Mary to get pregnant. She received God's desire by agreeing with Him and confessing her faith aloud, with words. God

# NOW FAITH!

will not force anything on us. By faith, we can receive anything that His Word says He wants to give us. Do you agree with this by faith? Do you believe we can receive anything God says in His Word He wants to give us?

So, we need to practice what we speak, and speak what we practice, and practice what we declare, and declare what we practice, and say what we preach. Is that merely a broken record? I don't think it does any good to teach people this in public if we're not doing this in private. I believe God preached what he practiced. I believe God practiced what He preached.

Let's read Scripture from Romans 4:13 where Paul writes, "The promise to Abraham and to his descendants, that he would be heir of the world was not through the law, but through the righteousness of faith." Guess what? If we're living the faith, the world is our inheritance. How's that possible? God's Word can't lie. How will that play out? Not by our ability to keep rules, but by our willingness to accept God's Word by faith. "For if these who are of the law are heirs, then faith is made void and the promise nullified. For the law brings about wrath. But where there is no law, there's also no violation. For this reason, it is by faith in order that it may be in accordance with grace."

LORD God, enable us to grasp the depth of grace! Amen? I've been trying to articulate new definitions of grace. I have attempted many times, but my best effort so far is this: **Grace is God's willingness right now to use His power, His ability, and His influence on our behalf, even though we don't deserve it.** Come on! Grace is God's willingness: this is what he wants to do. Grace is God's willingness right now, in this moment, to use His power, His ability, and His influence on our behalf, even though we don't deserve it. As we are reading this, do we want and need more grace? When we're filled with faith, we are enabled to live in grace. So, the promise keeps building! If we stay in faith, we become righteous. If we live in righteousness, we are enabled to live in grace. If we live in grace, the promise will be guaranteed. What does that mean?

The LORD guarantees His promise to all His descendants. "Not only to those who are of the law (or born as Jewish people physically). But also, to those who are of the faith." That would include us! "Also, to those who are of the faith" of Abraham, who is the father of us all. As it is written, 'I have made you a father of many nations in the presence of Him whom he believed. Abraham believed God who gives life to the dead and calls into being things that do not exist." Remember, God practices what he preaches. God told Mary, "You're going to have a son. He's going to be My Son". He spoke that divine Son into human existence on earth. Do you see it? He practiced what he preached. But he needed Mary to agree by faith.

Every person in the Bible did something we cannot explain. They agreed with what God said He wanted to do through them or for them! It's amazing: "in hope against hope." That would mean Abraham lived in faith because faith is the substance of what we hope for. So, when there was no hope in the natural, in hope against hope, he believed, so that he might become a father of many nations, he might become what God called him. He had to believe to become what God said he already was "according to what had been spoken. So shall your descendants be! Without becoming weak in faith, he contemplated his own body now as good as dead since he was about 100 years old." And the "deadness of Sarah's womb" in this story of miraculous faith is almost like Mary's story. It's almost like Elizabeth's story. It seems to me that God likes to birth newness. Do we see this? God wants to birth unusual newness by faith!

In the natural at age 100 and through Sarah's dead womb, there seemed to be no place for Abraham to find hope. He had to receive and believe his hope from God's words. We may be looking at a situation with family, or body, or finances, or emotions, or business.

# NOW FAITH!

We might ask, "Where am I going to get hope?" Well, if we cannot find any hope in our natural situation, why don't we go to what God's Word says about our situation? We'll always find hope in the Word of God. Amen?

Yet, "with respect to the promise of God, he did not waver in unbelief, but grew strong in faith." How is that possible? For 25 years he kept growing stronger in faith while his wife kept getting older in years. That requires some believing what God says beyond what his circumstance showed. Will we agree to hear and believe what God says instead of what our circumstances cause us to fear? He was "fully assured that what God had promised, He was able to perform. Therefore, it was also credited to him as righteousness."

Do you know what a righteous person looks like? From God's perspective, a righteous person is fully persuaded that God's Word is a greater reality than personal circumstances. Let's turn to Romans 10:6 and read, "Righteousness based on faith speaks as follows. If you're living the faith, you become the righteousness of God, and this is how you speak. Do not say in your heart, who will go up into heaven, that is to bring Christ down. Or who will descend into the abyss that is to bring Christ up from the dead?" In other words, we should not ask God to do something that He's given us the authority to do. Again, we should not pray, "God come down, rend the heavens and come down and help us" when He's already living inside of us. In other words, to be righteous disallows our circumstances to cause us to make religious statements instead of righteous speech.

This is so subtle. Come on! Some pray, "Oh, God help us!" when help and hope already lives inside us, waiting for us to release it. What does the LORD say? "The Word is near you in your mouth and in your heart." There we learn a perfect sequence: God puts His Word in our mouth so we can plant it in our heart. God actually put His Word in our mouth so we can say it and it can go into our heart. "That is the word of faith, which we are preaching: that if you confess with your mouth Jesus as Lord and believe in your heart that God raised Him from the dead..."

Remember, we must say it to get it into our heart. We confess with our mouth, so we can believe it in our heart. When we believe in our heart that God raised Jesus from the dead, we will be "sozo," we will be saved. "For with the heart a person believes, resulting in righteousness." That's the faith: with our heart, we live the faith. And with our mouth, we confess, resulting in salvation.

If we will commit to speak right words in the right way, we will experience unlimited possibilities of salvation. Amen? When we agree with everything that salvation provides, and say it aloud, we can actually start partaking and participating in an experiential reality of everything the blood of Christ has already provided. Whoa!

In Hebrew Scripture Psalm 107:20 we read that God sent His Word, healed us, delivered us, and saved us. How did He practice what he preached? In the Hebrew Covenant, He spoke and gave His Word to prophets or to angels to deliver messages. Wise kings searched for a prophet or seer and declared, "We want the Word of the Lord." So, in the Hebrew Covenant the LORD spoke. But how did He practice what He preached?

To answer that, let's ponder John 1:1, "In the beginning was the Word." The LORD was thinking about what He wanted to say. "In the beginning was the Word and the Word was with God and the Word was God. He was in the beginning with God. All things came into being through him. And apart from Him, not even one thing came into being that has come into being." Now we move forward to verse 14: "And the Word became flesh and dwelt among us. So, we saw His glory, the glory of the only Son from the Father, full of grace and truth."

## NOW FAITH!

So, how did God practice what He preached? In the Hebrew Testament for 4,000 years, He preached with His words. He preached holiness, righteousness, deliverance, salvation, forgiveness, atonement, healing, and provision with words. Then he said, "Now I'm going to practice what I preach." He empowered His Word to influence Mary's agreement in the Spirit, so that His words could manifest and become flesh by her "now faith"!

Let's think deeply about this. The LORD and His Word is what Jesus preached. He became the message in the flesh. He tells us through some of Paul's writings that if we believe His message, we can become living epistles. Our lives can actually preach the gospel of the Kingdom in words, actions, thoughts, and prayers. God enables us to re-present the Word made flesh. Jesus was the Word made flesh. We're supposed to practice what we preach like the LORD practiced what He preached. Jesus was the Word with God before time, but the Word (Jesus) became flesh when Mary spoke with faith and the Word became Yeshua/Jesus.

When the Word of God was revealed as Jesus, what did the Word made flesh look like? It was Acts 10:38. "He went around doing good, healing everyone that was oppressed of the devil, because he was anointed with the Holy Spirit in power and God was with him." That is amazing news! That is good news!

Also in 1 John 3:8, we learn, "The reason the Son of Man was manifested was to destroy the works of the devil." So, this is the same truth the Word fulfilled through the Spirit from heaven in the Hebrew Covenant. Then, that same Word came in the flesh, to show us what the Word in flesh form could and would do.

Think about the power of the spoken Word out of heaven. When millions of people left Egypt, not one of them was sick, not one of them was weak, not one of them was tired. They were all delivered by the power of the spoken word. Then that spoken Word became flesh. He showed us in flesh form that the same power through a word spoken out of heaven can be released in and through a Person speaking on the earth. There's no end to the power of the Word!

The Psalmist in 110:1 reminds us, "The LORD says to my Lord, 'Sit at my right hand until I make your enemies a footstool for your feet." I believe the LORD God is waiting on us to live the faith and for us to live in our authority and our true identity as the body and bride of Christ. As sons and daughters of the Most High God, we are the body of Messiah! Somehow mysteriously in the Spirit we are the body of Christ. I believe He is also waiting on us to destroy the works the devil so that all of His enemies will become a footstool under His feet.

I think the LORD wants us to participate in biblical family tradition. What blesses us as a daddy, or a mama, or a grandpa, or a grandma? This is what blesses us: to see our offspring becoming and doing what the LORD said a family should become and do! Do we agree that it makes God's day to see His children believing they have the same power in their words that was in Jesus' words? And they live in faith, they use their authority, they release their words in faith, and miracles happen, change happens, breakthrough happens, and salvation results! I think that makes God's day!

There is as much power in the Word of God in us as there was in the Word that was made flesh because He is the same Word. Can we get our minds around this? There is as much power in the Word of God in us, if we're willing to speak it, as there was when the Word was made flesh, because He is the same Word. That's why Jesus said in John 14:12, "If anybody believes in me, then the same things I do that person will do and even greater."

Is your heart burning like my heart is burning? I'm not realizing this fully yet. Brothers and sisters, I have tasted little glimpses of this.

But honestly, I am not realizing fully what my potential is. And you probably feel much the same. So, in Romans 10:9-10 we discover, "If you confess with your mouth, Jesus is Lord and believe in your heart that God raised Him from the dead, you will be saved. For with the heart a person believes, resulting in righteousness. And with the mouth, a person confesses, resulting in salvation."

When we speak what we really believe, faith springs to life. We can believe in our heart and be saved. We can become righteous, we can confess faith with our words, and we can experience salvation. Do we remember what salvation includes? It's such an all-inclusive package and the powerful picture is painted by Psalm 103: forgiveness of our sins, cleansing of our sinful nature, deliverance and freedom of our mind, and healing of our physical body. There are gifts, protection, guidance, fruit, longevity, prosperity, and eternity! This is an all-inclusive package called salvation.

If we need deliverance and healing, we need to start using our words to speak God's Word. Amen? When there is an area of our life we're struggling in, we need to use your lips to speak God's Word. Inspired by the LORD, the prophet Isaiah wrote in 54:17, "No weapon that is formed against you will succeed and you will condemn every tongue that accuses you in judgment. This is the heritage of the servants of the Lord and their vindication is from Me, declares the LORD."

Words are spoken often against us, by satan or a demon, from a person, from a colleague, from a family member, from a boss or co-worker, from a neighbor, or from a deceived world system. If those words are contrary to the Word of God, then our immunity, liberty, and birthright as believers, as sons and daughters, and as the Body of Christ retains authority to tear down those words and lift the Word of God in their place. Come on! No word spoken against us that is contrary to the Word of God has any right to prosper in our lives. We can believe and speak God's Word and allow God's voice to prosper in our lives. Isaiah 54:17 is an amazing verse! So, we need to lift our voice to speak God's Word with faith and confidence.

Let's return to Romans 4:16, "For this reason, it is by faith..." To speak God's Word sheepishly, or out of repetitive routine, or merely human method, or self-made positive thinking, or mental assent, or transcendental meditation, or yoga, and so on will not accomplish anything significant or lasting or produce any good. We must declare God's Word by faith, intentionally, boldly. We need to believe God's Word much more than anything else we believe.

Again, "For this reason, it is by faith in order that it may be in accordance with grace..." Grace! Oh, imagine what will happen when we remain and abide in grace and faith as the catalyst for our words! If we could stay in faith and let faith in God and His Word provide inspiration for our words! Then, we are living in grace. Again, grace is God's willingness to use His power, ability, and influence on our behalf, even though we don't deserve it. Do we hear that? Even when we don't deserve it, which is every time, all the time!

So, let's listen and embrace another gripping truth from 2 Corinthians 12:9, "The Lord said to me, 'My grace is sufficient for you, for My power is perfected in your weakness.' Most gladly therefore, I will rather boast about my weaknesses so that the power of Christ may dwell in me." When we realize that grace is God's willingness right now, to use His power, ability, and influence on our behalf when we don't deserve it, what else would we want God to say other than "I'll give you my grace"?

"By grace through faith" is the LORD's answer to anything we're facing! Most people are taught grace is, "Just hold on. You simply must go through this. God wants you to suffer, because if you can suffer, you become more like God." No! That's not grace. Grace is His power! Power to become totally dependent on grace through faith.

## NOW FAITH!

We must not become totally dependent on our ability to repeat Scriptures. We must no become totally dependent on our ability to memorize or receive communion or mumble a prescribed chant. Come on! Pagans do that! When we stay totally dependent on God, that's faith. And that's the realm of grace. That's the life in which all things are possible. To the one who believes!

The Lord is asking us to be willing to become weaker so we can live stronger. That might sound counterintuitive. The Lord is asking us to become more vulnerable so we can become invincible. The Lord is asking us to remove anything we think we can pretend with such as degrees, money, beauty, or false pride. He wants us to allow Him to clothe us with His righteousness and His glory.

Abram lived 24 years after God told him he would become a father of nations. After 24 years, the LORD changed his name to Abraham. This is significant. As long as his name was Abram, he and Sarah could not fulfill the promise to become a father of nations. But the moment the LORD changed Abram's meaning to Abraham, he fulfilled God's promise to become a father of nations. The moment Abraham started to profess with his mouth his new name and identity, the very promise God gave him 24 years earlier, he and his wife celebrated her pregnancy.

The moment Mary said, "Let it be done to me according to your Word," she became pregnant. Neither one of these examples was coerced. Abraham had waited 24 years: all he had was faith. Mary said, "I don't understand how this is possible, but I'm going to believe your Word." All she had was faith! None of it was emotional manipulation, nor was it was a methodology. Both of these persons were examples of total, vulnerable, transparent, authentic faith in what God's Word had spoken.

The LORD inspired Abraham to confess the Word that God had spoken over him, so God could perform his desire through Abraham.

I want us to read Isaiah 55:11, "So will my Word be, which goes out of my mouth. It will not return to me empty, without accomplishing what I desire and without succeeding in the purpose for which I sent it." When God's Word actually becomes our word, His desires can be fulfilled in our life! Then, His Word becomes the two-mouth sword. When we have remained in Him until His Rhema remains in us, when we have lived in Him, when our pursuit is only Him, and when our desire is Him until His Word becomes our reality, then we can ask Him for whatever (John 15:7).

Many people have manipulated this teaching into selfishness, but that's a doctrine of demons. I don't want anything, except the ability to introduce more people to Jesus. If I could fulfill that passion and mission, I wouldn't even want a vehicle. If I knew I could arrive where I needed to preach Jesus, I wouldn't want a vehicle. I wouldn't want a house if I could get by without it. I have no human desire for anything except a God-given ability to reach millions of people for Jesus. Because God can and will do what He says, I want to speak His words until I believe them. Are you with me?

As Psalm 105:17-19 summarizes: Joseph received and believed the word of the LORD. He had to wait 13 years in a prison. How did he survive? He held on to the Word. He never grew bitter. When his circumstances were opposite the Word repeatedly, how did he thrive? He kept believing the Word. Then suddenly, he was elevated and promoted as second in command of Egypt. From the pit to the palace, right? He ran out of the dungeon to run the nation. How? He never stopped holding on to the LORD and His word. Verse 19 notes that the word of God refined him until the word proved true!

According to Romans 4:18, "in hope against hope, Abraham kept returning to the word to get hope. He couldn't go to circumstances to receive hope. Many of us are holding on to situations for our son, daughter, or grandchild, our spouse, our church, our business, our

## NOW FAITH!

health, our finances, our emotions, or whatever or whoever else. We can hold on to the word of God if we keep going back to the word...if we keep going back to the word...if we keep going back to the word. We will not grow weary in well doing, but we will grow hopeful in faith to faith to faith to faith. It impossible for us to grow weary in the Father, Son, and Holy Spirit.

We remember Hebrews 11:1, "Faith is the substance. Faith's substance is what we're desiring. Faith's substance is what we're hoping for. Faith is the evidence of what we can't see yet. That's how real God's Word must become to us. Do we agree?

Abraham needed to choose God's Word over his 100-year-old body. While I am decades younger than Abraham was, many days, I preach and minister from 9:00 am until 9:00 pm. And during intensives with Prisoners of Hope at IHOP-KC, I pour out the energy of the LORD 12 hours daily for three days in a row. How? I must believe God's Word over my body.

Romans 10:17 reminds us, "Faith comes by hearing and hearing by the Word of the LORD." Think about this: Abraham did not have Scripture. Neither the Hebrew Covenant nor the New Covenant were written yet, so he could not seek guidance there. You know what? We don't have any excuse. Abraham received power from the LORD to keep saying what God said he was. I am Abraham. I am Abraham faith. By faith in the LORD, even without God's written word, Abraham knew who He was because He knew the One who had spoken to him. This is the power of saying what God's Word says.

Later, after the word of God was recorded by Moses, his successor Joshua wrote in 1:8, "Be careful to not let this book of the law depart from your mouth but meditate on it day and night. And be careful to do all that is written in it. So, you'll make your way prosperous, and everything to which you put your hands will be successful." What was the key God taught Abraham? What was the key God taught Joshua? What is the key He teaches us? We must live in words of the LORD, meditate on His words, believe His words, profess His words, and speak His words until His words become our reality. Then, our life will be significant and successful.

This is a picture of salvation from the Hebrew Bible. Salvation is wholeness and prosperity of our spirit, soul, and body. That is salvation. So, God was teaching Abraham and Joshua to live the faith. What the LORD is teaching us is the same: live the faith and live by faith. We believe, then we say what we believe. We declare what we believe. Confessing is saying what God's Word says about us. This is not trying to be selfish or boastful. This is not trying to get personal gain to build our personal empire. That's not faith. That's a doctrine of demons. That's religion. Faith is believing what God's Word says often enough and sincerely enough, that we can say it, because we believe it. We are not closet Christians. We confess and profess faith in God's Word publicly. That's faith. We need to start saying what God's Word says about us. Amen?

Now, here is our final challenge for this chapter. Faith is not established overnight. Faith must be established over time. It's a process. We can only start where we are. We can't start where others are, regardless of how well we know them or how deeply we respect them. We can't start where Billy Graham was, or Oral Roberts was, or where John G. Lake, Randy Clark. Bill Johnson, or Reinhardt Bonnke were. We have to start where we are. And who will walk with you? Jesus Christ, who is full of grace and truth and who grants faith as a free gift.

I want to live the faith by faith! Do you? Sincerely? Totally? Now? I want to speak God's Word, because He fulfills it, honors His Word, and it produces a bountiful harvest. I want to declare by faith until some barren woman gives birth. I want to declare by 25-year faith until God fulfills His promises. I don't care how long it takes. By God's grace

# NOW FAITH!

and favor, I am going to proclaim breakthrough until it happens. You can call me crazy, but I will live by grace through faith all the way to Judgment Day. I believe God's Word. I believe everything the Word says is ours through the blood of Jesus. The Lord says we receive by faith. He is waiting on us to believe.

I want to pray a prayer of faith. Let's agree together.

Father, thank You that You really live inside us through new birth in spirit, soul, and body. Thank You that You are not a far-off God or a false God. You are alive inside us. You're in our thoughts. You're in our dreams. You're in our desires. You're standing with us in our fears, waiting for us to lean closer to Your heart where there is no torment, and only shalom.

Now, Lord, I release a new measure of faith into my brothers and sisters: that we will live in You, where perfect love casts out all fear. There is no fear in love. We can and will live in you and Your perfect love. So, we don't have to fear sickness, or failure, or disease, or provision. In You, we don't have to fear. We can live in perfect love by faith in Your Word.

Father, I release this faith now into this reader. We want to receive and believe Your authentic gift of faith today, repeatedly, as we complete our responsibilities. You are blessing my brothers and sisters with the reality of Jesus Christ in them. Everything they need for life and godliness is in them right now: love, joy, peace, their healing, their deliverance, their provision, their prosperity, everything that You know they need. It's in their heart right now, waiting to be fulfilled when they confess what they believe. Hope starts right where we are now. We declare by faith together: we believe. We will say it until we see it. In the name of Jesus. Amen!

# 6

# PRACTICING DAILY RELATIONSHIP IN THE LORD BY FAITH

This is our sixth message on faith in the Word of God. Beyond this, the Lord has given me six more messages on faith. Together, we will learn much more from the Living Word, Jesus Christ!

At the end of the previous chapter on faith I noted that we have to start where we are. For example, when we want to build something, we cannot start by building the fourth floor when all we have is a vacant lot. We have to start by digging down in that vacant lot to solid ground, which is native soil or rock, but not fill dirt that sinks under pressure. So far, are we agreeing, and can we apply this spiritually?

To include a basement, we need to dig deeper. Then we can construct forms and pour footers to support heavy, concentrated loads. Footers provide a wider and stronger base for a foundation. On a foundation and sill plates we can start constructing a frame. We have to start from the bottom up, to start from where we're at. Eventually, as we start to build upward, we need to step first on the lowest rung of the ladder. We can only start where we are, learning to live faith in the Lord and the Word.

We should not read a book or hear someone's testimony and say, "I want to start where they are." Some zealous people hear testimonies of faith, and suddenly they think that's what they're going to do.

There's a big difference between faith and presumption. Faith is not like writing a million dollar check and believing God will cover it by the time it hits your bank. That is not faith. That's presumption. We need to be very deliberate to establish our faith on the Word of God. Each of us needs a firm foundation on words from Jesus, disciples, prophets, and other Spirit-inspired Bible writers.

Also, we need to establish our health, a safe home and food for our family, our finances, and maintenance for our car. We must collaborate the brain in our head with the mind of Christ in our soul and the worship center in our spirit. Each of these must be in partnership with our own personal faith right where we are.

We need common sense with our faith. That's why God gave us all a brain. We should be forever learning to live in the Spirit and to live in the world simultaneously and harmoniously. We can't substitute faith with good business practices, and we can't substitute good business practices with faith. That is also true with good ministry practices or good family practices. Faith should be something that is a part of what we do, not separate from what we do.

Every aspect of our life should be an act of worship and should be fulfilled in faith. "The righteous shall live by faith!" That means we should live everything in our natural life and everything in our spiritual life without disconnection and by faith. Additionally, we cannot be in faith and keep looking at our circumstances all the time. If we find ourselves in circumstances contrary to the Word of God, then it is not possible to focus incessantly on circumstances and live by faith simultaneously. Our focus needs to be continually fixing our eyes on Jesus, hearing His Spirit, receiving the Word of God, and believing. Do you understand and agree?

We don't negate our circumstances. We don't lie about them. We refuse to say they're not real. We earnestly, honestly acknowledge

# NOW FAITH!

there's a greater circumstance. There's a greater reality. Reality that's eternal. Reality that can't fail. So, we need to keep speaking what God's Word says. We need to keep thinking and doing everything like Jesus thinks and does.

Here's an example. Way back in the Garden of Eden, Adam and Eve surrendered their God-given authority to an angel called Lucifer, who manifested as a serpent. They empowered him to become the prince and power of the age. Because mankind gave up authority, satan seized power. The LORD spoke to Adam, Eve, and the serpent with come-to-Creator-counsel. God said a time would come when a woman's seed would crush satan's head. The LORD worked diligently 4,000 years to fulfill that prophecy. Why so long? It took 4,000 years for God to convince enough people to hear Him speaking His words and to obey and cooperate with Him.

More than 300 prophecies about the Messiah were spoken out of the mouths of humans who had authority. Now, we can study through Hebrew Scripture (the Old Testament) and hear prophecies of where Messiah would be born, a virgin who birthed Him and in what specific town, whose son He is, the tribe He's from, the region He's from, and what He would be called. All those needed to be spoken by people who had God's authority. The LORD chose to speak His desire with words to people. Similarly, if we want something to happen, we will need to speak God's Word with faith in God's authority over our circumstances.

Are we hearing, receiving, and believing that theme as we go through this series of messages? Again, we cannot merely assimilate ideas by osmosis or practice transcendental meditation, assuming something will happen solely because we're thinking it. To accomplish something significant, our thoughts have to produce words. Words are the capability God created and demonstrated to release power. Words release power. Power to live and power to die. Power to inspire hope or produce despair. Power to encourage or discourage. Words are the catalyst of the life we're living. Come on!

Proverbs 18:20 teaches, "We eat off the fruit of our lips." In other words, the life we're living is a product of the words we've been speaking. Again, the life we're living is a result or fruit of the words we've been speaking.

So, God spoke prophetically through people for 4,000 years before He was born as a baby. The final word that allowed Him to be born on Earth was spoken by a young lady named Mary, "Let it be done unto me according to your word." She had to come into agreement and alignment with the word of authority God spoke. Her words illustrated the law of faith.

Now, let's practice saying what we believe. Let's speak aloud together Mark 11:23 where Jesus taught, "Truly I say to you, whoever says to this mountain, be taken up and thrown into the sea, and does not doubt in his heart, but believes what he says is going to happen, it will be granted to him."

I wrote this down. In essence, Jesus said, "You can have what you say if you believe what you say." Jesus said that and Jesus can't lie. He doesn't exaggerate. He doesn't stretch the truth. Jesus said, "We can have what we say, if we believe what we say." That includes all things that we declare. So, we should always be speaking what we desire, which means we should always be speaking God's words. The only words that don't return void are words that start in God's heart, then come through our heart and mouth, then go back to God's heart. Please read that last sentence a few more times until you perceive, receive, and believe.

Matthew 5:37 is another amazing verse. Jesus said if we actually believe, then our "Yes" can be "Yes" and our "No" can be "No". Imagine

## NOW FAITH!

what will happen when we believe our words are so simple and real? For instance, on one afternoon recently, I scheduled a prayer appointment at 1:00 with one person. Then, at 3:00 I had a prayer call with a person to believe and declare healing from cancer. Immediately following that at 3:30, I started yet another prayer call with another person to proclaim Christ's healing authority over cancer.

I often trust and believe the LORD to empower me while I pray over the phone with people who need to be healed. He enables me to say, "No, cancer: you cannot live. Now, friend, yes! Be healed by faith in the name of Jesus." Do we believe that our "No" and "Yes" by faith in Christ is enough? Do we base that faith consistently on the power of God's Word in us? Can we believe that His Word is authority? Our "No" means "No" and our "Yes" means "Yes."

In other words, without trying to build a case, we could be like Mary in John chapter two. Jesus was a guest at a wedding in Cana of Galilee when the bridal couple ran out of wine for their guests. Mary informed Jesus about their need and asked Him to help. Then, He turned to His disciples and said, "Do whatever He says." He turned water into the best wine of the night and the best of many weddings. Mary didn't argue with Jesus. She knew He could do what He said. What if we agree in what He can do? What if it had nothing to do with how we were feeling emotionally? What if it had nothing to do with how we were doing circumstantially? What could happen if we actually believed God's Word has the power that it says?

Do you see why I am so intrigued with this theme of faith? I seldom see Jesus getting really emotional, except one time when He turned the tables over in the Temple because the salesmen were desecrating the holy place. He showed anger then, but that was against religion. His anger wasn't against problems such as sickness or disease or storms or lack. His anger was against religion. I do not think Jesus was awakened on that boat when the storm was going to sink the boat because He was afraid. I don't think He became extremely passionate. He yawned and declared to the wind and waves, "Peace, be still." He believed the power of His words. And I believe He wants us to grow up and become like He is. Do we want to grow up and be like Jesus?

Now, please hear my heart. I don't want to discount emotional engagement because emotion is how we experience passion. I get it. God loves our passion. That's why He gave it to us. He gave us our feelings, our emotions, so I don't want to disengage. I just do not want emotions to have any ability to talk us out of faith. I don't want our feelings to have any ability to talk us out of the confidence that God's Word will do what He says. So, we need to believe God's Word.

Let's look at Romans 4:21: "He was fully assured that what God had promised He was able to perform." We need to become fully persuaded that God's Word can do what He promises. Because every word of God is a promise; it can't lie. God's Word is not a book of lies. It's a Book of Promises.

We need to be assured that Joshua 1:8 is a verse on which we are willing to stake our eternal existence. God spoke to Joshua, "Do not let this book of the law depart from your mouth. Be careful to meditate on it day and night. And be careful to do all that's written in it. Then, He will make your way prosperous, and everything you touch will be successful." The LORD was teaching Joshua how to live by faith, because "faith comes by hearing the Word." And the best way to hear the Word is when we hear it from within our heart, our own thoughts, and from our own mouth. When we hear the Word from our own mouth, it goes into our inner ear, which is our spirit gate. God's Word is imprinted more deeply when we hear the Word in our own voice.

When Dr. Craig Rench and I traveled together, he showed me that the phrase, "Be careful to meditate on it day and night" features a

## NOW FAITH!

Hebrew word translated "murmur or talk to yourself." "Be careful to meditate and speak this word day and night!" Remember: this is what a cow does when it chews the cud. A cow bends down and grabs a big bite of grass and then stands up and starts to chew. The cow just starts chewing and chewing and mooing. Then the saliva mixed with the greens and nutrients go out of the first stomach into the second stomach.

The cow keeps chewing and swallowing and the second stomach sends the nutrients into the third stomach. Then, out of the third stomach into the fourth stomach. Finally, the fourth stomach makes cow piles and steak. Go figure! Grass produces cow patties (manure) that most of us dislike and steak that most of us love. God created cattle to be able to digest and extract every bit of nutrients from grass. God also created our hearts to be able to chew and chew and meditate, murmur, and talk to ourselves, and extract every bit of life from every bite of His Word.

You know, sometimes I allow my mind to slow down to focus on one verse or one paragraph or one chapter for weeks or months. God created us to be able to digest the Word, to extract truth, to meditate on Him, to believe and receive healing, to get revelation, life, vision, and anointing out of every syllable that He ever spoke into existence. We could, if we would be willing to chew on it day and night, day and night, day and night, day and night. Do we agree that there is that much power in the Word of God?

Now, let's turn to Deuteronomy 28 and revisit a scenario from the last chapter of the Pentateuch, the first five books of the Hebrew Bible. Deuteronomy 18:1 is similar to and a precursor to Joshua 1:8. Look at what the LORD teaches in Deuteronomy 28:1, "Now, it shall be that if you diligently obey the LORD your God, being careful to do all his commandments which I am commanding you today, that the LORD your God will put you high above all the nations of the earth." What do you think about that? Does that sound good? You might respond, "Well, those were Jewish people in the context of Moses delivering them from bondage in Egypt." I get that, but we are grafted in. We're a part of the body of Messiah. That's our grace also: we have been grafted into that same people so "the two will become one."

If we agree, let's keep hearing, receiving, and believing these verses in Deuteronomy 28 that are our reality and that backup Joshua 1:8, so we can be effective, productive, successful, and prosperous. "These blessings will come to you and reach you if you obey the LORD your God. Blessed will you be in the city and blessed will you be in the country. Blessed will be the children of your womb, the produce of your ground, the offspring of your animals, the newborn of your herd, and the young of your flock. Blessed will be your basket and your needing bowl. Blessed will you be when you come in. Blessed will you be when you go out." How blessed do we want to be? More? Let's continue.

"The LORD will cause your enemies to rise up against you to be defeated by you." In other words, the LORD will let them think they have a chance so you can defeat them. "They will go out against you one way and flee from your presence seven ways. The LORD will command the blessing for you in your barns and in everything that you put your hand to. And He will bless you in the land that the LORD your God has given you. The LORD will establish you as a holy people to Himself, as He swore to you if you keep the commandments of the LORD your God and walk in His ways. Then, all the peoples of the earth will see that you are called by the name of the LORD, and they will be afraid of you. The LORD will give you more than enough prosperity in the children of your womb, in the offspring of your livestock, and in the produce of your ground in the land which the LORD swore to your fathers to give you.

"The LORD will open for you His good storehouse: the heavens to give rain to your land in its season and to bless every work of your

# NOW FAITH!

hand. You will lend to many nations, but you will not borrow. The LORD will make you the head and not the tail. You will be only above and not underneath. If you listen to the commandments of the LORD your God that I am commanding you today, to follow them carefully, and do not turn aside from any of the words that I am commanding you today, to the right or to the left to pursue other gods or to serve them." All those blessings are a result of hearing and doing the word.

Then, in Deuteronomy 28:15-68, we see 54 verses of curses. I don't want to read verses about curses right now, but I encourage you to read them. Remember, those apply to us if we don't obey and live the Word. In Deuteronomy 30 the LORD says, "I set before you blessings and curses." He gives us the choice: life or death. Life is in the Word. Come on! The Word is spirit and life. The Word of God produces spirit and life. Death is in disobedience to the Word.

So, if we are fully persuaded that God can do what His Word promises (Romans 4:21) and we are willing to meditate on it day and night, never letting it leave our mouths, and we are careful to do all this written in it (Joshua 1:8 and Deuteronomy 28:1), then we can and will receive all the blessings in our lives that are listed in Deuteronomy 28:2-14. That's God's promise! If we don't obey His Word, then we will need to endure and suffer under all the curses in verses 15-68. This is a no brainer! We should do what the LORD says every time, all the time! Let's say what He says and do what He says! Let's obey God's Word. Are we willing, ready, and able by faith?

Let's look at 2 Peter 1:1, "Simon Peter, a bond servant, and apostle of Jesus Christ, to those who have received a faith of the same kind as ours, by the righteousness of our God and Savior, Jesus Christ. Grace and peace be multiplied to you." Now, let's pause there a moment. Remember our definition of grace? **Grace is God's willingness to use his power, influence, and ability on our behalf even though we don't deserve it**. That's grace (Greek: charis).

Peter writes, "grace and peace." Now peace is a word for wholeness, an antidote and antitoxin for any selfish contamination and spiritual infection in our hearts. Peace is the atmosphere of heaven. Jesus said, "My peace I give you." He has given us a piece of peace, a touch of triumph! That is what we will enjoy for eternity and starting now by faith: no more striving, no more sorrow, no more sickness, no more disease, no more separation, no more loneliness, no more delay, no more pain, no more tears, and more! Peace is huge. Peace is what grace is trying to produce in us. If we receive and believe that principle by faith, let's personalize and say it aloud: Peace is what God's grace is trying to produce in me and us!

Peter wrote, "Grace and peace be multiplied to you." We want to know how that can happen because we want shalom, we want peace. Right? The word here for peace is not shalom, but it is the Greek rendition for the Hebrew word shalom. Peace is in the knowledge of God and not in our striving, not in our suffering, not in our sacrifice. Do we want this grace and peace to be multiplied to us? We receive both grace and peace one way: in the knowledge of God, in knowing the Lord personally.

How else are we going to know God? Really, how are we going to know Him? We can converse with Him: listen and talk. We can pray in the Spirit. We can gaze on Him and meditate on Him. I get all of that and so do you. But He also gave us His Word, this Book of Promises. He poured a lot of effort and authority into assembling and protecting the authorship and the manuscripts. He gave us a Book to know Him, more than to know about Him. There's a difference: His Word is not a biography about Him. This Book is different. This is a heart connect: to know Him in Person, personally! He designed His Word for one reason, one purpose: so we can know Him. He wants us to grasp, receive, believe experiential participation in His very life!

Let's continue, "Grace and peace be multiplied to you in the knowledge of God and of Jesus Christ our Lord. His divine power

# NOW FAITH!

has granted to us everything pertaining to life and godliness." Divine power! Let's think about that phrase. Life is our temporary physical life. Godliness is our eternal life. And God's power has given us everything we need for both our 70, 80, 90, or 100 years of physical life as well as our unlimited eternal life by faith now! It's already been given to us by God's power. It's already His grace-gift to us...as we receive and believe!

Again, listen to this: "His divine power has granted..." It's His gift, granted it to us! "He has granted to us everything pertaining to life and godliness." That means everything we'll need in this life: the answer we need in business this week, the answer we need for our future, the answer we need in our health journey, the answer we need for emotional well-being, the answers we need in every aspect of life. He has already given all of this and more! Amen?

"Everything pertaining to life has already been granted to you." How? "Through the true knowledge of Him who called us by His own glory and His excellence." So, the more we know him, the more we experience what is already ours. But we don't pursue things. We don't try to solve symptoms; we pursue the Source. We don't run after the promises; we pursue the One who gave them to us. I'm not saying we should avoid desiring miracles. That's not the point.

Here's the point: we need right motives and right sequence. Daily, we practice intimate knowledge and relationship with Him. Then, all those things that have already been granted to us become our reality in our true knowledge of Him. We see that in 2 Peter 1:4, "Through these He has granted to us His precious and magnificent promises." That's the whole Word of God, "so that by them you may become partakers of the divine nature." We have the written Word that always leads us to the Living Word. The written word always leads us to the Person that inspired the written Word.

So, we live by faith, which is hearing the Word, seeing the Word, gazing into the Word, and receiving the Word. But we have to start in the Word to get into the Word. It's the law of faith. Oh, we need to embrace this! Grace and power promises all that is wrapped up in knowing Jesus personally. Not merely head knowledge, but head and heart knowledge combined. Pharisees had and still have a lot of head knowledge, but they don't know Jesus personally. The Devil boasts a lot of head knowledge, but definitely does not want anything to do with grace by faith in Jesus. The Lord wants our head and heart to become one in pursuing knowledge of Him. With our head we are always yielding to the mind of Christ in our heart. With our natural mind we always yield to the mind of Christ in our spirit. Always. He wants that kind of pursuit of knowledge, not knowledge that puffs up, but knowledge that builds up.

I am sincerely trying to reveal the Word slowly enough that all of us grasp the truth by faith. That's the goal of Isaiah 40, the prophet says we will soar, and we will run, but we end up walking. I'm trying to walk because I never see Jesus running. The life of faith is not so much a life of soaring and running. It's normally a life of walking. Every place we place the sole of our feet we take the Kingdom of God. We receive that place as part of the domain of what our faith possesses. From Isaiah 30:15, we learn this faith is not in striving, but in resting and trusting.

Note in Hebrews 1:3, "He is the radiance of His glory and the exact representation of his nature." Let's examine slowly the word "representation." That's the same Greek word as in Hebrews 11:1, "Now faith is the substance of things hoped for." The word "substance" and this word "representation" come from the same Greek word. Jesus is the actual substance of our faith. He is everything our heart desires: healing, safety, peace, freedom, prosperity, dominion, authority, confidence, and more! Jesus is that substance. "He is the exact representation of His nature and upholds all things by the

Word of His power. And when He had made purification of sins, He sat down at the right hand of the Majesty on high." Notice His word is His power: "by the Word of His power." What did His power provide? It provided more than forgiveness for the guilt of our sins, what we have done. His power provided purification of our sinful nature, what we are. His power provides forgiveness of sins and holiness of heart and life! All by now faith.

He is the solution! His grace is longing to produce His peace in every aspect of our life: our health, our hearts, our emotions, our family, our relationships, our ministries, our business, our city, our nation, and more! His power is producing His desire in every aspect of our lives!

Here is a little revelation that I received from the Lord in my heart not long ago. Isaiah 53:5 has become one of my favorite verses in the Bible: the Lord was "pierced for our transgressions, He was crushed for our iniquities, the punishment that brought us peace was on Him, and by His wounds we are healed." That's the verse from which we teach "Prisoners of Hope" Intensives at IHOP-KC. Line one is our forgiveness, line two is our cleansing, line three is our deliverance, and line four is our physical healing. Of those four lines, we are liable only for line one. We need forgiveness because of transgressions, intentional disobedience to the Lord and His Word.

We're not guilty for who we are, because we were born in sin due to the rebellion and disobedience of Adam and Eve. That's the devil's work. We're not guilty for emotional dysfunction because of the way our parents abused us or for the way the evil one enslaved us from childhood. This caused us to live in fear or shame or bad vision of ourselves: never good enough and always incapable or insufficient or ineffective or unproductive. We are not guilty of that. That's a part of "falling short of the glory of God", but we are not guilty for that. And we're not guilty for physical sickness, unless it's a result of sins for which we need to be forgiven, such as lung cancer from smoking packs of cigarettes each day. Then, that's something we are responsible for. But if we are plagued by sickness because of the sin of Adam and Eve, we're not guilty of that.

This is the grace of Jesus for us and in us. Jesus came to forgive us for our own guilt and shame so He can free us from the bondage of everything the devil has done. This is so important. We are responsible only for the first line of those four lines listed above. Jesus is the solution for everything the devil is trying to do to take us out. He is the solution for all that. And it starts by the Word of His power!

The Lord upholds the whole universe in place, and His power provides purification of our sinful nature, our character. Jesus destroys the work of the devil so that everything in us now produces life instead of death. This is such a big revelation. In 1 John 3:5 we see the reason Jesus came was to forgive our sins. I'm thankful for that. Then in 1 John 3:8 we see another reason he came: to destroy the works of the devil. I am deeply thankful for that, aren't you?

So, the Lord's divine power is His Word. And His Word is His nature. Our knowledge in His Word increases His power in us, His promises for us, His nature flowing into and through us, and His influence in and through our lives. As soon as we believe the knowledge of His power, then we receive it. That is when we can declare with confidence, "I believe!" That is when we can live the Mark 9:23 reality, when Jesus looked at the man with a sick son and said, "If you can? All things are possible to the one who believes." I sincerely believe that promise is still intact and in play today. I believe that promise. I understand some the nuances of it so far and want to grasp and practice even more.

My brothers and sisters, I experience the same struggles you face. For instance, the director of IHOP-KC asked me recently to teach and

# NOW FAITH!

lead a 20-minute ministry of healing at Forerunner Church. I shared a few promises from the Word of God, several testimonies, and a half dozen words of knowledge.

As I released words of knowledge, I said, "Now if these words of knowledge are touching your body and you're feeling the symptoms leave, I want you to come forward. Well, people filled the whole front of that auditorium and were instantly healed by Jesus by His words of knowledge flowing through me. Again, they were healed instantly.

One lady, crippled since I've been ministering at IHOP four years, walked up without the cane she needed to use for at least all those years. Another lady whose knee joints were bone on bone testified to zero pain in her knees. I heard people declaring testimony after testimony of what the Lord had done in those moments.

A few days later, I went to the coffee shop next to IHOP's prayer room. A lady who served coffee said, "I was healed of insomnia." When the Spirit gave me words of knowledge the previous night, I had said, "Many of you haven't slept in years. That is never going to be a problem ever again." She said, "Dan, I don't know how to explain this. I could not sleep soundly for so long. But after the Lord touched me, then all three nights on Friday, Saturday, and Sunday, I slept through each night. I didn't wake up one time! I was healed by the Lord through a word of knowledge!"

Now, I don't understand how some people receive instantaneous healing, while some other people contend for healing for decades. I don't understand that. I want more knowledge of Him. If the grace, the faith, the promises, and the power are in knowing Him, then I don't have "Plan B. I want and need to know Him more. I must know Him more! Amen?

Not long ago, I was preparing to travel to Korea to preach the Word of God. I was hoping He would give me Korean language. My father-in-law and mother-in-law had to study that language for years when they ministered there, but I was hoping the Lord would manifest that Acts 2 gift in me so I could speak the language of those people. Also, I wanted and needed a new hip. I bought a new cane, but I didn't know whether the Lord would give me a new hip for that trip. But I did know there would be hundreds of miracles of healing.

I don't understand how the Lord heals, except that He pours His grace through His gift of faith when we declare that faith. I do not yet understand whether healing flows from first-fruit faith, or whether people are not familiar with each other, or whether they respond with childlike innocence. I don't understand healing completely yet, but I am understanding little components of healing. I do know that Jesus did not experience some of the same struggles most of us experience because of His intimacy with the Father. I am pursuing and deeply desire to receive that depth of intimacy in Christ with the Father. Again, brothers and sisters: I know the same struggle you face with the same pursuit and with the same grace through faith!

Here is my motivation in teaching on faith: I want to become one with Jesus. I want to become one with Him in a God-given way, so He is glorified. God sent a Person to flow through. That's my heart: I want Him to flow through me also. "So, all things pertaining to life and godliness are ours in the true knowledge of Him!" I want the true knowledge of Him and authentic faith in my mouth and in my heart. Do you get this, friends? Do you long for Him also?

This is what Paul wrote in Romans 10:8, "The Word is near you, in your mouth, and in your heart. That is the word of faith that we are preaching." I think Paul is the greatest apostle of all time. He is the greatest apostle ever sent with a message of revelation of the Messiah and His Kingdom. His revelation featured a few key pillars. Number one was faith. Number two was grace. Number three was righteousness. And number four was "say it." That is a simple summary of Paul's whole revelation.

# NOW FAITH!

We are His Body. We receive His grace through faith. We are His righteousness. So, we should start saying it and release that reality into every circumstance of our life. It all revolves around the Word, not the feelings. Paul led worship and preached while processing heavy, hard emotions. He delivered his greatest sermons in the worst of situations. His power had nothing to do with circumstances. It had everything to do with his love for Jesus, his fullness in the Spirit, and his confidence in the Word of God. By grace through faith!

Friends, a time is coming when our circumstances are going to erode rapidly, when things we thought were secure disintegrate, fall apart. How and why do we know this? Because the Bible is true. We must live by faith now based on God's Word. Period, full stop.

Do you feel this urgency and imminence burning in your heart? Do you sense that we will need to stand on the Word: it's in our mouth so we can put it in our heart? And it's in our heart so we can release it from our mouth? This re-presents the power of God's nature, which is His Word. That's the law of faith. God's nature and power is in His Word. His nature is his power. And his power is His Word. Now, we have access to that Word. We should never stop meditating on it day and night. Can we say this a thousand different ways so at least one will stick?

Jesus teaches us in John 15:7, "Abide in Me until my Rhema abides in you. Then, you can ask whatever you want and it will be given to you." We can and must abide in Him until His Word becomes our word. Then, we can ask for whatever we want and it will be given to us. What do you think of abiding in Him? Remember, He's the goal. He's the prize of abiding in Him until His Word abides in us. Jesus did not say we could ask for whatever we want, but it will be disappointing to us. He promised, "It will be given to you." He provides amazing benefits to this walk of faith, friends!

Now, let's apply 1 John 3:20-21, "If your hearts don't condemn you..." When we ask, we need to know we are asking within God's will, that we are aligned with God's Word. We cannot just say, "I want my neighbor's house to burn down because I want that lot." That's not faith; that's greed, pride, and perversion. We need a heart that does not condemn us. None of what we're learning together will work if we're not aligned with the Word of God. We must always start with the Word. We must live in and through the realities the Lord and His Word are trying to produce. Our heart cannot condemn us when we begin to ask God for something. If our hearts condemn us, we will not receive. Amen?

In 1 Peter 1:5 we discover we are "protected by the power of God through faith for the salvation ready to be revealed in the last time." Remember that salvation is the result of our faith receiving God's grace. There's no end to what salvation produces in us. If we remain in faith regardless of the circumstances until salvation is revealed in these last times, then we can become a beacon of hope, an oasis of safety, a lighthouse on a hill, a lamp on a stand, and so on. All this can become reality if we live by faith. The world is looking for hope and people living in faith and by faith have a lot of hope to give.

We can rejoice in 1 John 5:14-15, "This is the confidence we have before Him, that if we ask anything according to His will, He hears us. And if we know that He hears us in whatever we ask, we know that we have the request we've asked from Him." This is the way to live: knowing that all we ever ask is what God's Word says He wants to give us. That's called living the faith. That's called living in the law of faith.

I meet with people every single week who are struggling with their finances, worried about adequate provision and their future. Luke 6:38 is a solution for that: "Give and it will be given to you pressed down, shaken together, and running over. People will give into your

# NOW FAITH!

need." One Sunday morning I was invited to preach at a church in Harrisonville, Missouri out in the middle of the country. Most of the entire congregation are partners with our ministry because the pastor believes in Becoming Love Ministries and wants everybody to sow financially into our mission and vision.

This pastor was adopted as a baby, so he has a heart for orphans. He got a vision from God to run a marathon every day to raise awareness for homeless kids and others that need families. When I was there, he had just finished running his 107th marathon in 107 days. He had been running 26.2 miles every day for 107 days. He set the world record for men and women. And I asked him, "Are you hurting yourself?" He replied, "No, I'm running only four miles per hour. I'm not trying to run fast. I'm just trying to keep going."

Well, he got up and prayed over my trip to preach in Korea. He prayed that 100,000 people in those 300 churches of influence would birth revival together in Korea. Then he prayed that those Koreans would give one million dollars for our water wells in Africa. I recognized in my spirit the anointing on his prayer. And the Lord filled my heart with faith and anticipation.

In Genesis 8:22 the LORD promises, "While the earth remains, seedtime and harvest, cold and heat, summer and winter, day and night shall not cease." As long as there are seasons, as long as there is day and night, and as long as we're still on the planet, breathing oxygen, and gravity still works, seed time and harvest will produce. Whatever we sow, we will reap. If we sow words of healing, we'll reap a harvest of healing. If we sow words of fear, we will reap a harvest of discouragement and fear. If we sow financial seeds, we'll reap a financial harvest. As long as humans are alive, that law of seed time and harvest is working. God's Word is true and cannot lie.

So, whatever we need, we need to plant it. What do you need? We need to plant it because a seed always produces what we need. Seed always fulfills our need. So, what do we need?

As we close, please receive and believe James 1:22, "Prove yourselves doers of the word. And not just hearers who deceive themselves." If you merely read these messages and take notes, but you don't practice grace through faith, you have not yet received, and might be deceived. We must do what it says.

The word "doer" is the Greek word "poi-e-mo". Scholars propose many definitions. Here is my understanding: if we are going to live the faith we need to perform or put into practice the script that's been given us. And the script that's been given us is the Word of God. So, to avoid being deceived, to live in freedom and prosperity spiritually, physically, emotionally, and to enjoy eternal life that Jesus' blood has provided, then we need to be doing the Word. That's living the faith: doing the Word. Do you get it? Doing the word.

The way we reap a harvest is to plant. We have to plant something. We walk in love, in humility, in forgiveness, and in an unoffended heart. We don't let pride and jealousy and envy and strife exist. Come on! Let's walk in love, in humility, and in forgiveness. Oh, I wish I could say that enough times that all of us would actually hear it. Walk in love. Walk in humility. Walk in forgiveness. Walk in love. Walk in humility. Walk in forgiveness.

Finally, we will have the confidence to say like Mary, "Do whatever He says." Then, water will be turned into wine. Loaves and fish will be multiplied. Storms will be calmed. The dead will be raised. Blind eyes will be opened. And we will be living in the law of faith!

# 7

# GROWING FROM FAITH TO FAITH THAT ACTS AND WORKS

We are learning together through 12 chapters how to live in Christ by the law of faith, that is by His grace through faith. Let's continue in Hebrews 10:23 and "Let's hold firmly to the confession of our hope without wavering, for He who promised is a faithful member." Much of our study in the Word of God so far has focused on "faith comes by hearing." Our current verse in Hebrews is a reminder that we have to hold on to faith. What we're confessing is what helps our faith grow. We must hold on to our confession, what we're saying. We need to hold firmly to the confession of our hope.

We remember: faith is the substance of what we hope for. Because the substance of our faith is our confession, we should be confessing what we're holding on to. This is verse reminds us that faith is a journey. Faith is a lifestyle. Faith is a process. It's not a method or an equation to get results, although faith does produce results. Faith is a perspective for life now, to live daily, momentarily. In this way, we become more and more like the One our faith is fixed on: Jesus.

So, we need to hold fast to the confession of our faith. Our faith will rise no higher than our confession of God's Word. We need to say what God's Word says, and not what the devil says. What's coming out of our mouth should be what came out of God's mouth, not what the devil said. During circumstances, symptoms, delays, or distractions life in the world causes, we should not repeat or rehearse in our minds, emotions, or words that satan twists and distorts. We should be declaring over ourselves and others what God's Word says: it's truth and life!

Confessing with our words is to faith what thrust is to an airplane. I'm very thankful that thrust works. In 2023, I flew on a plane from Kansas City to Seattle to Seoul, Korea. Our flight time from Seattle to Korea took 12 hours in the air. But when we flew back, the same course took only a few minutes more than 9 hours because we had a tailwind. The plane worked well partially because of thrust. Remember? Thrust is the power that pushed us and kept us air born. Our confessing and professing the Word is the thrust it takes us from glory to glory to glory to glory. When we stop confessing the Word, we lose the thrust that lifts us higher in the Spirit. Romans 10:17 teaches us, "Faith comes by hearing and hearing by the Word of Christ."

Now let's claim Psalm 45:1, "My heart is moved with a good theme." May I ask: what moves your heart? We remember that "out of our heart flow all the issues of life." If it's a good theme, we'll address our words to the king. In other words, we will start repeating God's Word back to the LORD.

The Psalmist adds, "My tongue is the pen of a ready writer." So, when we use our mouth to confess God's Word, we cooperate with Him to write His Word on our hearts. Our tongue is the pen that is writing God's Word on our heart toward the goal. Our goal is that out of the overflow of our heart, we will speak and sing the Word continually. The more we speak God's Word, the more the Word will help us define and develop who we are, our character, our identity. Amen?

Faith always sees. Faith always believes. Let's declare that aloud together! Faith always sees. Faith always believes.

## NOW FAITH!

The International House of Prayer in Kansas City (IHOP-KC) started practicing this 20 years ago and continues daily during 24/7/365 Bible-based prayer and worship they broadcast globally via live video. There, many pray God's Word, sing God's Word, and meditate on God's Word. Many similar Houses of Prayer have learned to do this now all around the world.

In 2 Corinthians 4:18 Paul wrote, "We look not at the things that are seen, but at the things that are not seen. For the things that are seen are temporal. But the things that are not seen, are eternal." So, when we focus on things to show up in the natural, they will never be based on faith. They will be based on what is natural and totally temporary, which means things and situations in our lives will go up and down, up and down, up and down. However, if we rivet our perspective on God and our eyes fixed on Jesus, on what His Word says and on what the Truth says, then we will go and grow from faith to faith and from glory to glory.

Faith gives the human spirit the ability to conceive the seed of what God's Word will produce. And that's the law of faith. God's Word can't lie. God's Word is seed and our heart is where we need to plant it. If we will continue to plant it, and not doubt it, the Word of the LORD will produce the harvest it was sent to produce. Remember: when faith starts, it is always in seed form. The kingdom of God is like people who sow seed. We don't sow full-grown trees. We sow seeds: our words. Our words are our seeds, like God's Word is His seed.

We never develop fully-grown faith all at once. In Mark 10:15, Jesus reminds us that we need to receive the Kingdom of God like a little child." While we are born again by grace through faith in an instant, we do not grow in the King or His Kingdom all at once. We receive Kingdom lifestyle little by little. We need to start with what we have, just like a child, and grow from there. Nobody starts in the journey of faith with the whole Bible in their heart. But each of us starts with what we have in our heart. Do we understand and agree?

Paul reminded the Romans and us in 12:3, "God has given all of us a measure of faith." When God gave us the initial seed of faith in new birth, we received a gift of faith through His Word in our heart by reading the Bible ourselves or by hearing someone teach us. Then, the more we plant the Word in our heart, the greater the measure of faith we have to grow, to enjoy and to share with others. Many denominations in Christianity are missing whole segments of the Gospel of the Kingdom that are not part of their narrative. Many have not yet received revelation of grace through faith that is not of ourselves. When we pursue and embrace the whole counsel of God's Word in our heart, then we have the measure of faith He wants us to enjoy, believe, grow, and declare for others.

It's up to us to plant the Word. It's up to us to sow the seeds of God's Word so that our measure of faith sprouts, matures, and flourishes in the grace that God entrusted to us. We touched on this in a previous chapter based on Ephesians 2:8, "We are saved by grace through faith." Grace has already been given to us. Better yet, all of God's grace has been given to us! If we will keep developing our faith in Jesus closer, deeper, stronger, and higher, we can experience and enjoy more and more of Him and His Spirit in complete salvation.

Salvation is not merely forgiveness so we can go to heaven. God's provision of salvation is the whole, all-inclusive package of His love, grace, and faith: peace of mind, the prospering of hope, of dreams, of influence, of authority, of enablement to be and do what God wanted us to be and do from the beginning. All of that and more is available to us when we cooperate fully with God to build our faith. Salvation can continue to grow because all God's grace has been extended to all of us in Christ Jesus. He did not withhold any grace from any of us.

# NOW FAITH!

The more faith we're willing to develop by planting the Word of God in our heart, the greater the growth, progress, and joy in salvation we will experience. Amen? Eventually, we will profess and possess everything the Lord offers and provides because growth is eternal. He is waiting on us and leading us to develop our faith. Faith in action is God's personality in manifestation. Faith in action now is God's personality in manifestation. Let's revisit Hebrews 11:6, "Without faith, it is impossible to please Him. For the one who comes to God must believe that He exists. And that he proves to be the One who rewards those who seek Him."

The law of faith is the law of God. The law of faith by works was the Old Covenant. And the law of faith that works is the New Covenant. In Romans 3:27, "Where then is boasting? It has been excluded. By what kind of law? Of works? No, by the law of faith. So, the covenant that we're in now is the covenant of the law of faith, not the law of works. To live by the faith is to live in the covenant that the blood of Jesus provided for us. Again, in verse 27 we see that boasting is excluded by the law of faith. Then, in verse 31, Romans asks, "Do we then nullify the law through this faith? Far from it. On the contrary, we establish the law." That's the law of faith that the Word teaches at the end of verse 27.

So, the law of faith, the principle of faith, and the perspective of faith, is what Jesus asked about in Luke 18:8. He wanted to know whether He, the Son of Man, would find people living in this new law of faith when He returns. Do you know why He asked that? Because it's so easy to give up on faith and go back to worry, back to fear, back to works, and back to flesh. Why do we go back? Because faith is unseen, unfelt. Faith is unprovable, except by the Word of God. To live by faith means it's all of faith. It's either all of faith or nothing of faith and all of works.

I often remember Romans 14:23 where Paul writes, "Anything that doesn't come from faith is sin." I am so glad God has forgiven us of all of our sins, aren't you? Are you glad that the moment you believed in the grace and the blood of Jesus, He forgave you of all your sins? Many people many times on many days think or say things that don't come from faith, because they return to declaring, "Well, I don't know how God is going to do this, so I need to help Him right now." That was not faith. But aren't you glad God has forgiven us, so we don't have to focus on past sin already confessed, repented, and forgiven? We can focus on grace and faith as we become more like Jesus. We can grow up and become more like Christ. The Word and the Spirit are nudging some of us now, right? "Yes, Lord, we are listening and agreeing!"

Faith that works is the law of the New Covenant. Hebrews 11:1 teaches, "Faith is the substance of things hoped for and the evidence of things not yet seen." That's the new covenant law of faith that is a substance. It's tangible! It's based on what we're hoping for. So faith is what we desire. If we're not desiring what the Word of God says is ours, we won't be able to remain and grow in faith. Does that make sense? We cannot be desiring things contrary to the Word of God and stay in faith. Faith has to be based only on the Word. If we can match our desires to what the Word says is ours based on the blood of Jesus, then we can stay in faith because the Word remains forever. Come on! But if we're trying to fulfill desires outside the Word, we're not living by faith. Instead, we're living by selfish ambition.

Next, let's add Hebrews 1:1-3, "After God spoke long ago..." Let's stop there a moment, after God spoke His words. Remember in the Old Covenant, God sent His Word and healed them (Psalm 107:20). So, even in the Old Covenant, God's word was His voice. He was speaking. That was His word. Again, "After God spoke long ago to the fathers in the prophets, in many portions, and in many ways, in these last days He has spoken to us in His Son." Eventually, He spoke His

# NOW FAITH!

prophetic words about the Living Word, Jesus. The LORD practiced what He preached, He spoke things into existence, including His Son, who was and is and is to come: the likeness of Himself. And the Word became flesh and lived awhile in our neighborhood.

Now the Word, the Son, is the message of the Father. So, the message is not only the spoken word. The spoken word produced the Word made flesh. His message is what the Word made flesh is, the substance of faith. Mysteriously, all of us who have received salvation by grace through faith are the Body of Christ. We are the Word made flesh. It takes all of us--all the Koreans, all Americans, and all the faith-filled people around the world to be the body of Christ. We need each other because we can't function without part of the body.

Let's continue in Hebrews 1: "...in these last days He has spoken to us in His Son, whom He appointed heir of all things to whom He also made the world. And He is the radiance of God's glory, the exact representation of His nature, and He upholds all things by the Word of His power." The whole universe is held in place by the Word. That's His power! Since His Word is in us, every time we speak His Word, He pours again His power that holds everything in place.

Let's review a word in Hebrew 1:3 that we mentioned in a previous chapter: "He is the radiance of God's glory, the exact representation of his nature..." That word "representation" comes from the same root as the word "substance." In Hebrews 11:1 where we read, "Faith is the substance", the same word appears here again in Hebrews 1:3 as "the exact representation." It's the same word. So, Jesus, in essence, is the substance of our faith. Jesus is the exact representation of God and what our faith is made of. In the end, He is everything we desire.

Jesus is the desire of all nations. That's why when we listen to His Word, our faith is planted and grows as we gaze at Him and become like Him. Our faith is perfected and grows because He is our desire.

He is all we are hoping for. He is the prize. He is everything. What He does for us includes all the benefits that come with the prize. So, in essence, faith is the inward journey of becoming one with Jesus. That's faith! And there's more. Eventually, we can't distinguish where our spirit ends and where His Spirit begins. We are one in the bond of love!

Then, God's substance is Jesus. Faith's substance is Jesus. That's why Jesus said in John 10:30, "I and the Father are one." And that's why Jesus said in John 14:9, "If you have seen me, you have seen the Father." Jesus said that He is the Word made flesh and manifested, which is the law of faith demonstrated.

Imagine what our testimony can become when we really practice faith in Christ as a principle, we never quit or deny Him, but we keep growing and drawing closer to Him? Until with Jesus, we can say, if you've seen me, you've seen Jesus. If you've seen me, you've seen the Father. I and the Father are one. Isn't that the goal of faith? Come on, brothers and sisters! Isn't that the goal of faith? So that when they look at us, they no longer see us?

In Psalm 17:15, we read that as we grow in faith and Christ, one day we will look in the mirror and will no longer see ourselves. We will see the One living in us and "be fulfilled in His likeness." Don't you love that? We have unlimited possibilities of living the faith! Doesn't this make your heart long and burn for greater intimacy with Jesus? 1 John 3:2 agrees, "We know that when He appears, we will be like Him, for we will see Him as He is." That's the faith goal.

In John 12:49-50, Jesus said, "I did not speak on my own. But the Father Himself who sent me has given me a commandment as to what to say and what to speak. And I know that His commandment is eternal life. Therefore, the things that I speak, I speak just as the Father has told me." Recall that Jesus said, "If you've seen me, you've seen the Father. I and the Father are one." Paul wrote that Jesus was the fullness of the Deity dwelling in bodily form. The writer to the Hebrews said that Jesus is the exact representation of the glory of God. He is the message of God.

So, Jesus lived the manifestation of the personality of God in flesh by saying only what God was telling him to say. Remember, if we are living by the law of faith, we're manifesting the personality of God. Jesus is the personality of God. And all Jesus said was what the Father told Him to say. He lived faith. He did not say flippant or careless words. He said exactly what the Father told Him to say. Hal Perkins is teaching moment by moment by moment by moment by moment we say only what Jesus says to say and nothing else. That is the goal of faith. Because all that Jesus tells us to say produces precisely what those words say...if we believe.

Jesus is the substance of things hoped for. Jesus is God's Word in human form. Jesus is God's Word in bodily form. Paul wrote in Colossians 1:19, "It was the Father's good pleasure for all His fullness to dwell in Christ." So, all the fullness of God is in bodily form in Jesus. And all Jesus says is what the Father says. John 5:19 adds that all Jesus does is what the Father does. Living by faith cannot be merely our words. Faith has to include our actions backing up our words. That's why we say that the New Covenant is faith that works: faith in action.

The Bible teaches that as Jesus is, so are we in this lifetime. The Bible also teaches that the goal of redemption is that all of us grow up to the full measure of the stature of Christ Jesus. So, do we believe, without being "wigged out" or "weirded out", that eventually we should be like Jesus in spirit and soul? Do we believe we should be able to do what Jesus did? By grace through faith, should we be able to multiply food, calm storms, walk on water, raise the dead, walk through walls, and our presence would heal people?

Do we believe these are some of the goals of becoming one with Jesus? Do we believe these characteristics describe part of the faith of the bride Jesus is longing and waiting for? Do we believe His bride needs to become like the bridegroom before He can return for her? Can we think of any way to do this outside of living by faith in Him and His Word? Is this making sense according to the Word of God? Some people might look at us and call us crazy, heretics, apostates, or whatever. But do we believe the goal of all Scripture is that God wants us to become like Jesus Christ? The LORD God actually wants us to become like His Son!

The LORD provides unlimited possibilities by faith! When we believe, what we can do in Him and with Him is unlimited. Colossians 1:27, "God wills to make known the wealth of the glory of the mystery among the Gentiles. The mystery is this: Christ is in you, the hope of glory." Let's think about that realm a moment. All that Christ is, is in us by faith now. Then, what is our responsibility? To practice and speak faith! How much are we willing to develop, practice, and speak our faith? All of Christ in us is waiting to manifest through us, based on how much we are willing to develop our faith! Amen?

So, how can we develop, practice, and speak faith in Christ who lives in us, the hope of glory for us and others? Let's think together about our personal "Acts of Faith" to cooperate with God. My Bible section heading at James 2:14 is "Faith and Works". That is in the right order. It's not works into faith. It's faith and works. Faith produces works. Faith actually works!

Now to James 2:14, "So what use is it, my brothers and sisters, if someone says he has faith, but he has no works? Can that faith save him? If a brother or sister is without clothing and in need of daily food, and one of you says to him, 'Go in peace be warmed and be filled,' yet you do not give him what is necessary for his body, what use is that? In the same way faith also, if it has no works is dead, being by itself."

I'll give you an example. During one of the 13 services we preached in Korea, I noticed that in my flesh, I couldn't flow as freely in words of knowledge, because I had to wait for the interpreter to finish. I could not communicate and connect in ways the Spirit has gifted me. As a result, I couldn't speak as many specific words of knowledge, and I needed to declare more general words. It was simply more challenging and time-consuming with an interpreter.

After one of the services, I was weary and wanted to go back to my room to rest. But the Lord said, "I want to heal some of these precious people, but I need you to demonstrate acts of faith and use your words to unleash the power." I heard The Voice and needed to cooperate. I had to declare my faith by works, right? So, I released one word, "Some people here have terrible feet problems. If you will stand up and jump now, you will notice the Lord has healed them." Not only did I need to practice faith and act with words, but also the people had to act on their faith. Very quickly, a dozen people jumped, then testified that their feet were healed by jumping, by doing what the word said, and all the pain left their feet.

On another occasion, the Lord gave me a word that people whose hearts were out of rhythm were going to be healed. By faith, I spoke that word and 13 people came forward. By the time we were done placing our hands on them, all 13 of those precious Koreans declared aloud that their hearts were at rest, they could breathe more easily, and their hearts were restored to right rhythm. If we will receive and believe God's word spoken to our hearts, declare that word with faith, then practice acts that correspond, the power of God can manifest. We cannot expect God to accomplish anything unless we act and express that faith. We can expect God to accomplish what He spoke to us when receive, believe, and act on His words with faith.

This is why we love the Book of Acts. We receive faith as a gift from the Lord and invest it right back into the Lord. By obeying Him, loving people, and declaring truth. Faith acts. Faith works.

The Lord speaks impressions into our hearts continually, waiting for us to act and practice an obedient expression. This is our reasonable act of faith. Let's keep reading in James 2, "But someone may well say, 'You have faith and I have works.' Show me your faith without the works and I'll show you my faith by my works. You believe that God is one. You do well; the demons also believe and shudder. But are you willing to acknowledge, you foolish person, that faith without works is useless? Was our father Abraham not justified by works when he offered up his son Isaac on the altar? You see that faith was working with his works. As a result of the works, faith was perfected."

Isn't that interesting! Some parts of us still need perfecting, even though our spirits are perfect. Our souls and bodies need to be perfected, waiting on us to do acts of faith, so they can agree and align with our spirit. While our spirit may be perfect in faith, our mind and our body might lag behind our spirit. That is why we need to practice acts of faith.

Let's continue in James 2:23, "And the Scripture was fulfilled which says, and Abraham believed God, and it was credited to him as righteousness. And he was called a friend of God. You see that a person is justified by the works and not by faith alone." We must keep faith and works in the right order. If we attempt works while trying to get into faith, that's law. But if we live by faith and practice works with faith, that's grace on display! Isn't that amazing? It works!

Now back to James 2:25, "In the same way, Rahab the prostitute was not justified by her works when she received the messages and sent them out by another way. For just as the body without the spirit is dead, so also faith without works is dead." See that order? First: faith.

# NOW FAITH!

Second: without works...is dead. Faith with works is alive. Faith works in that order.

Faith requires a response, which is always obedience to what God's Word is saying. So, we need to act out our faith, to the measure of faith we have developed. Our faith is dead if we're not willing to love and help others. Then, it cannot thrive internally. Ultimately, faith must transform people with needs for the edification of the Body eternally. God is not interested in superstars. God is committed to the Bride of Christ becoming just as He is. We should check our motives, whether we're in love or not, because the law of faith works only through agape love. Remember, this is the new commandment: that you love. So, faith is only God-type faith if it is working as Jesus-type love. Amen?

Let's turn back one chapter to James 1:21: "Therefore, ridding yourselves of all filthiness, and all that remains of wickedness, in humility receive the Word implanted, which is able to save your souls." That's the goal of faith. Remember 1 Peter 1:9 teaches us that if we'll stay in faith, we'll receive the goal of our faith, which is the salvation of our soul. Our soul includes our will/decisions, our mind/thoughts, and our emotions/feelings. We need forgiveness and cleansing in both our spirit and our soul.

We need the Word implanted, the Word implanted, the Word implanted in our spirit, soul, and body. Then, we must prove ourselves doers of the Word and not just hearers who deceive ourselves (James 1:22). Let's reiterate this in many different ways. We cannot merely sit around speaking the Word if we're not going to implement and act on what we're saying. In other words, we must practice in faith what we proclaim about faith. We must practice acts of faith that back up our words of faith. We cannot merely say "I'm going to become healthy because I'm going to start confessing the Word of God." When we speak faith, we must put faith into action by putting healthy food into our body. We must activate our faith in practical ways for others and ourselves. We must become doers of the Word. Do you agree?

"If anyone is a hearer of the word and not a doer, he's like a man who looks at his natural face in the mirror. For once he has looked at himself and gone away, he has immediately forgotten what kind of person he was. But the one who has looked intently at the perfect law, the law of freedom, and has continued in it, not having become a forgetful here, but an active doer, this person will be blessed in what he does" (James 1:23-25). We want to be blessed, don't we? Then, let's do the Word.

So, we hear the Word, we say it, and we do it. We're blessed because God's Word can't lie. We want to share this message with every pastor and leader who struggles to motivate people to practice loving needy people, serving, giving generously time, talent, and treasure. The Lord can bless every pastor who practices these principles of faith so clearly and consistently that the congregation is drawn and challenged to be blessed as well by practicing faith that works. Each of us needs to keep looking into the perfect law, the spiritual mirror, the Word, which will reveal the way God sees us, not the way the devil sees us, and not the way people see us.

Now, let's allow God's Word through 1 Corinthians 13 to help us discern whether we are living by faith. Let's "examine ourselves to see if we're even in the faith." Living the faith is living the law of love. They're interchangeable. "The only thing that matters is faith that works through love" (Galatians 5:6). In other words, the conduit of how we live the faith is always through agape love: selfless, sincere, sensitive, Savior-like love.

Let's insert our own name in each description of love starting with 1 Corinthians 13:4: Dan is patient. If I'm not, I need more faith. While flying to Korea, missing a night of sleep, and feeling numb,

## NOW FAITH!

I realized again that I needed a lot more patience. In my soul (will, mind, emotions), I was "in and out" of rest, "in and out" of love, "in and out" of patience, and "in and out" of faith. The Lord showed me again that if I remain in faith with corresponding actions of patience, then eventually my soul can be so anchored in the Word and Spirit that there would be no "in and out" regardless of my circumstances.

That's how Paul and Silas could respond at midnight after being beaten and thrown into prison. The primary response flowing out of them was that they were full of love for God and patience toward their accusers. That produced worship at midnight, the goal of faith and patience when persecuted. We can become so one with God, that no matter what hits us, the only response that comes out is what fills us. That's the goal of faith. So, Dan is patient. Now, insert your name instead of mine and speak it by faith out loud.

Next, Dan is kind. Insert your name there again. Then, ____ is not jealous. ____ does not brag. ____ is not proud. ____ does not act disgracefully. ____ does not seek personal benefit. ____ is never offended. That's a lot to ponder, so let's pause there a moment. Do we want to be able to discern whether we live in and by faith? Are we easily offended? Now, repeat each of those above at least one more time before we move on. As you repeat, activate faith.

Next, insert your name here: ____ does not keep a record of wrongs suffered against self. ____ does not seek personal benefit. ____ never rejoices in unrighteousness but ____ only rejoices with the truth. ____ always has confidence. ____ always keeps believing. ____ always hopes for all things. ____ endures all things. We need to pause here again and repeat those by faith.

Here I illustrate again. When we got to the airport to depart Korea, I requested a wheelchair because I can't walk all the way through those airports with my painful hip. So, they brought a wheelchair to pick me up, but it was only large enough to crowd in one of my legs. Literally, I'm not exaggerating! That poor wheelchair was only the width of one of my thighs. So, I looked at it and exclaimed, "Well, that's not gonna work." Then, we had to wait about 30-40 minutes more for somebody to locate and bring a wheelchair that I could fit in.

I wasn't real patient because I was hurting, I had preached 13 times total, finally two times that day. Added to that, we had driven an hour to the airport, so I was exhausted because I hadn't slept the previous night, and my body was hurting. So, I was fighting to put action to my faith because I knew it was necessary for the perfecting of my soul and body. I knew that my spirit was perfect and that it could help perfect or at least console my soul. You know what I thought and felt. You've been there and done that sometime, somewhere, with someone.

Here is one final statement. Again, insert your name: \_\_\_\_ never fails. So, do we really want to get to the place where we can say we never fail? Would that be one of the ultimate goals of living by faith in relationship with Jesus Christ and faith that works in relationship with others?

Let's evaluate how we're doing in practicing faith that demonstrates love in whatever ways we need to serve each other. If we have areas where we're not in faith, let's start practicing them. Be patient. Be kind. Let's decide to do whatever it takes to get our soul and our body in agreement with our spirit and get back into living by faith that works. The goal is to live the faith and to hear from Jesus, "Well done, good and faithful servant." Right? That's the goal. The Lord wants each of us to practice corresponding actions with the Word for every circumstance. So, we need to decide to do what the Word says, to align with truth in the Word of God.

# NOW FAITH!

I have a lot of favorite Scriptures and Mark 4:26 is one of them: "Jesus was saying, 'The Kingdom of God is like a man who cast seed upon the soil. He goes to bed at night and gets up daily." I wish that would be easier. I didn't know how important that verse was until I suffered jetlag from the other side of the planet, about 12 times zones away from home. I didn't know how hard it would be to go to bed at night. Although my body cried out for sleep, my clock was 12 hours off, proposing it was time to get up at sundown and rundown. "He goes to bed at night and gets up daily and the seed sprouts and grows, how he himself does not know. The soil produces crops all by itself, first the stalk, then the head, then the mature grain."

So, we are responsible to sow the seed and to speak the Word. We need to profess what God says for divine energy to overpower our circumstances. Genesis 1:11 records that everything the LORD created already contains the seed within itself. Also, Luke 17:5-6 reminds us that if we "have faith as small as a mustard seed, we can say to a mulberry tree, 'Be uprooted and planted in the sea,' and it would obey us."

Do you remember that mustard plant seeds cannot be cross-pollinated? In other words, we cannot mix God's Word with other people's words. The only kind of faith that can move impossible situations is faith that comes only from the Word of God, without other words added that dilute it. We need to know, believe, and speak the pure, unadulterated Word of God. That must be our confession. We need to confess promises of God over needs we and others face.

Here is our final verse for this chapter. This is how we practice Genesis 8:22, "While the earth remains, seedtime and harvest, cold and heat, summer and winter, day and night shall not cease." Note the words at the top of the list before weather, seasons, and day-night cycles. The top of this list is a willingness to plant seed. When we practice planting, there will always be a harvest. God's Word is seed. The harvest multiplies even more seed, but we must first plant the seed of faith in the Word of the LORD God.

Are we willing to live by faith, holding fast our confession of hope? Will we commit to keep declaring what we're hoping based on God's Word? Will we never stop speaking words of faith? If so, He will provide a harvest from seeds we're planting by faith. So, we need to plant the seed, go to bed, and rest in shalom. We need to plant the seed and trust the promise. And when we get up, we need our faith to work for as many others as possible. Amen?

# 8

# ACTIVATING FAITH GROWS MORE FAITH

Foundational themes in this book include living now by faith in the Lord and the Word, as well as the power of our words to declare faith from our hearts.

In the previous chapter, we touched on James 2:17. Let's revisit this truth for emphasis and deeper discovery: "If faith has no works, it is dead, being by itself." So, we must add to our faith a corresponding action. Faith cannot be merely a theory or a thought in our mind. Faith needs accompanying action, or it's dead. If we have opportunity and ability to help someone, and we merely say, "Well, I pray you will be blessed", then we are not acting in faith. Again, we need corresponding actions with our faith, so that God's gift of faith actually lives and works.

Again, according to Mark 4:14, our heart is the soil, and the Word of God is the seed. Also, I keep reminding us of Genesis 8:22, "While the earth remains, seedtime and harvest, cold and heat, summer in winter, and day and night shall not cease." Yes, our heart is the soil. God's Word is the seed. So as long as the earth is still spinning and we are alive, God's Word can produce a harvest in our heart, if we will plant His Word. That's the law of faith that God put into place. Aren't we thankful for that? This principle has nothing to do with how we're feeling. It has nothing to do with what our circumstances seem to say. This is a law of God that He instituted.

Now, we repeat a challenge through a significant verse we declare in many places: James 1:26, "If anybody claims to have religion, but has not yet learned to bridle his tongue, he deceives himself." What does that verse mean? If our words are the seeds, and our heart is the soil, then words we say are the seeds we sow into the soil of our hearts. For example, let's ponder words such as, "I'll never get ahead. I'll never be healed. My relationship will never be restored. My ministry struggles and will never flourish. I'll never experience joy again. I'll never have prosperity." Then, our words are sowing seeds of doubt and despair into the soil of our hearts. And the LORD designed our heart to produce what we say. For clarity and emphasis: God created our heart to produce the seeds we put in it. Our words are seeds.

On the other hand, sometimes we converse in a group or declare to someone in need, "By His stripes you're healed. By the truth, you're set free. People will give to you pressed down, shaken together, and running over." As we say these or similar words, seeds of faith and hope are planted into our hearts. Then, the soil of our heart is confused and deceived because it doesn't know which seeds it is supposed to produce: the private words in secret or the public words on display. We need to guard our mouths, to guard our tongues. Come on! Life and death is in the power of the tongue. If we're speaking out of depression, fear, worry, envy, or bitterness, those words are sowing into our heart, seeds we don't want in our heart.

Remember, Hebrews 11:1 asserts that faith is the substance of what we want, the substance of what we're desiring and hoping for. So, we speak it. The way we sow it is to take action and speak it. We cannot merely think it. We must speak it. For example, Jesus took five loaves and two fish. He looked up to heaven. He spoke blessing over the meal. Then, he broke it and gave it to His disciples to distribute it.

# NOW FAITH!

Right? What was the corresponding action of faith in this story? The disciples actually did what Jesus said. Again, our faith always needs corresponding actions, words, and works. So, let's practice that: let's be doers of the word!

The *miracle* of faith: five loaves and two fish fed about 20,000 people and there were 12 baskets of leftovers. The *principle* of faith: Jesus spoke what He desired, the Word of God. Then, His disciples acted on it and kept distributing what Jesus told them to give. The power of faith-seeds is to act on those words. The *result* of faith: whatever a person sows, he or she will reap. According to Galatians 6:7, "Whatsoever we sow, we will reap. If we sow sparingly, we will reap sparingly. If we sow lavishly, we will reap lavishly." Amen?

Now, let's return to Mark 4:26 to review the law of sowing and reaping. Jesus was saying, "The Kingdom of God is like a man (*or a woman*) who casts seed upon the soil." The Kingdom of God in action is like us human beings casting seed in the soil. Remember: the soil is the heart. The seeds are our words. "The kingdom of God is like a man who casts seed upon the soil. He goes to bed at night and gets up daily, and the seed sprouts and grows, how he himself does not know." To live in the Kingdom doesn't mean we have to understand how the seed will produce. We merely need to understand that it is enough to go to bed and rest after we plant it.

Then, the soil produces crops all by itself. So, our heart automatically produces what we put in it. Automatically! That's how God designed us. Our heart automatically produces what we put in it. First, the stalk, then the head, then the mature grain, and finally the harvest. How do we sow seed? We speak, we declare, we say what we mean, and we mean what we say.

In Mark 11:23 Jesus was teaching Peter and the disciples how to declare power with their words like Jesus declared when he cursed the fig tree. Remember? Then, He said, "If anyone says to this mountain, be cast into the sea, and does not doubt in his heart that what he says is true, but believes what he says, he receives it." Amazing: the mountain obeys! Jesus modeled and taught that the way we sow seeds is to declare. We speak what we want, what we desire, always based on the Word and the Holy Spirit in our spirit.

Therefore, we should say, "Whatsoever we say, we will reap. Whatsoever we say, we will reap. Let's repeat that aloud now. Whatsoever we say, we will reap. And yet, some people keep saying, "That's not working for me." Then, what they're saying is actually happening: it's not working because that is what they declared. Come on!

How about this verse in Luke 17:6, "If you have faith like a mustard seed, you will say to this mulberry tree, or sycamore tree..." You will say to it, right? You won't merely think, merely hope, merely pray. You will say it, declare words with faith. "Whoever says to the mountain." "Whoever says to the mulberry tree be uprooted and planted in the sea, it will be done."

Again, until we get this. How do we plant seeds? We have to say it with our mouth. We have to say it with our mouth. Do you hear this with your heart? Do you receive this? How do we sow seed? We say it. We say it out loud, so our heart can hear our words. If a farmer plants seeds, and those seeds produce a harvest of what he plants, how much more will the Word of God produce when we decide to plant words of faith! Come on!

If a farmer goes out and buys a half million dollars' worth of wheat seed and he plants it in the soil, God has designed the soil to produce a harvest of even more wheat, right? Well, why shouldn't we believe that if we plant the seed of God's Word in our own hearts or other people's hearts, that it will produce better than natural seed? The

# NOW FAITH!

Word is incorruptible seed. It's pure, holy, trustworthy, imperishable, indestructible, powerful, productive, and effective!

In 1 Peter 1:23, we read, "You're born again not of corruptible seed but of the incorruptible seed of God's Word." Here, the word seed is "spore", which is a cell in a plant that enables reproduction. Also, 1 John 3:9 teaches that when we are born of God, born again, we must not continue to sin. The seed of God's Word in us and will guide away from sin. Here, the word seed is "sperma" from which we get sperm that also enables reproduction. These words describe in allegorical and metaphorical terms how seed reproduces in botany and how seed reproduces in humanity. In the same analogy, God's Word is seed that will reproduce after its kind in the natural world, in the physical world, as well as in the spiritual world. The Word will reproduce what is planted if we're willing to plant it. Got it?

So, God's Word is good seed. But many times, our confounding words perplex and deceive our hearts (James 1:26). Then, we don't see much or any of the harvest we long for, because we speak disconcerting or disorienting opposites. For example, I know people who have been taking prescriptions for 40 years, three times a day, because the doctor told them to, and they just keep doing it. It seems they have more faith in a prescription from man and medicine than the prescription of how the LORD and His Word supplies all our needs.

Also, I know Christians who will declare something one or two times and then give up on it. Why wouldn't we have as much faith in the Word of God as we do in the words of people? Why would we declare something with faith for a few days, then stop believing and start doubting or fearing again? Amen?

For those of who live by faith in the Lord and the Word, when we are sleeping, our spirit is in communion with God, because our spirit does not sleep. Follow this closely: "Faith comes by hearing" (Romans

10:17) and our spirit hears what we speak into it. We can plant the Word and words of love, faith, grace, and hope about ourselves and others into our spirit by speaking. Then, while we could go to bed so our body and soul can sleep, our spirit is producing the good seed all night long.

Note Proverbs 20:27, "Your spirit is the lamp of God, searching all the inward parts of our spirit." Our spirit never sleeps, never slumbers, and never shuts down, because our spirit is one with God who never sleeps and never slumbers. So, we can get the Word into our heart 24/7/365: 24 hours every day, 7 days every week, 365 days every year. Do we agree?

Now, let's read another favorite Bible passage. I know that you and I have a lot of favorite Bible passages because we love the Word of God. Here is 1 Corinthians 2:11-13, "For who among people knows the thoughts of a person except the spirit of the person that is in him? So also, the thoughts of God no one knows except the Spirit of God. Now we have not received the spirit of the world, but the Spirit of God who is from God, so that we may know the things freely given to us by God. We also speak these things not in words taught by human wisdom, but in those taught by the Spirit, combining spiritual thoughts with spiritual words." When we are born again, the Spirit of God moves into and inhabits our spirit, so our spirit becomes one with the Spirit of God. We are born again, born of the Spirit into new life in Christ. Then, we need to be cleansed and filled with the Holy Spirit.

In 1 Corinthians 6:17 Paul wrote, "If anybody joins himself to Christ, the two become one spirit." We become one spirit with God. Now, the spirit of a person knows the person. We know what God wants because we are born of His Spirit. If we will live by the Spirit and not by the soul, we will know what His Spirit offers and provides for us. Then, we can start saying it by faith.

# NOW FAITH!

However, if we are living only by our soul (will, mind, emotions), then we are motivated and moved by our own decisions, thoughts, feelings, circumstances, situations, disappointments, our hurts, traumas, real-time dilemmas, distractions, and so on. Then, we will speak words out of our soul, which have little or nothing to do with what God wants to give to us. How do we know this? Because God is Spirit, and those who worship Him must worship in spirit and truth.

Sisters and brothers, all of this goes back to the Word, because the whole Word is Spirit-born and Spirit-breathed. We want to know what God wants us to have: more of His Word and Spirit. Everything in His Word is for us. To speak the Word of the LORD into and over our lives results in unlimited potential. What we can "act-ually" accomplish by faith and fulness in the Spirit is unlimited. So unlimited!

Our spirit is designed by God to produce a harvest, a harvest that our Spirit produces even when we're sleeping. Philippians 4:19 encourages us, "My God will supply all your needs, according to His glorious riches in Christ Jesus." Christ Jesus is the Word of God. So, when we're speaking the Word, we're speaking abundant provision for all our needs. Again, "My God will supply all your needs, according to His glorious riches in Christ Jesus." Christ Jesus is the Word of God. If we're speaking the Word of God into our spirit and heart, into our needs, then we're speaking divine supply because Jesus is the Word, and He is all we need.

Let's illustrate this fact of faith with a different approach. Everything that mankind will ever need to live the LORD God Creator placed in the soil of the earth. That includes every fruit and vegetable humanity needed during the 6000 years or so until Jesus returns. The LORD also created every animal for meat, every tree for construction, every rock quarried for concrete, every mineral for health, every atom for atomic energy, every drop of water for hydration and washing, every piece of aluminum for building, everything from riverbeds for sand, all the oil, diesel, and fuel, and everything else that mankind needs to exist and thrive on this planet. God created all of this and so much more in the soil for us to utilize.

It's all in the soil. He doesn't have to put anything else in the ground that we'll need for life. In the Garden of Eden, He gave it to man and woman. He was waiting for us to harvest and capture what He created in the soil. All of this was waiting to automatically produce. That was the genius of God.

When we were born again, the Holy Spirit enabled our newly generated heart and newly blessed spirit to become the new Garden of Eden. So, everything we will ever need for eternity is in our new, born-again Garden-of-Eden heart, waiting for us to plant the seeds. Then, those seeds can automatically produce the grace God already placed in us. Jesus taught us to pray in Matthew 6:10, "Your Kingdom come, and Your will be done on earth as it is in heaven." Let's make that prayer of Jesus our very own.

How will His prayer be answered? We need to plant a seed. How is His Kingdom going to come? How is His will going to be done on earth as it is in heaven? It's all in us, because according to Luke 17:21, the Kingdom of God, the new Garden of Eden, the dwelling place of God's dominion has been planted inside of us. It's in our new, born-again spirit. Remember, "The Kingdom of God is not a matter of meat or drink, but it is of righteousness, peace, and joy in the Holy Spirit" (Romans 14:17). Right? The Kingdom is in the Holy Spirit: righteousness, peace, and joy in the Holy Spirit.

So, if we are living by faith in the Word and the Spirit, then everything we will ever need for life and godliness is already in us! Peter wrote in 2 Peter 1:3 that everything we will ever need for life and godliness has already been planted into our new Garden of Eden, Kingdom of God, soil of our heart. All of that is in us! Everything we will ever need for life and godliness is inside our heart right now waiting for us to plant a seed by faith, so it can automatically produce more.

Again, the Kingdom of God is in our spirit or our soil. And the soil has everything we need, just like the Garden of Eden had everything Adam and Eve needed. Now, we must plant the seeds. Nobody else can sow them for us. We have to plant the seeds ourselves. The Kingdom of God is like a man who goes around sowing seed. Jesus did not say the Kingdom of God is like a man who assigns somebody else to go around sowing seeds for us. We must plant the seeds.

We need to confess, profess, declare, pray, believe, and receive whatever we desire in agreement with the Master's will. In other words, as Jesus proclaimed in John 15:7, we need to abide in Him until His Word abides in us. We need to remain in Jesus until His Rhema abides in us. Then we can ask whatever we will, and He will give it to us. He has already put those seeds of faith in us by grace through faith in Him. Everything we will ever need for life and godliness He has already created and planted inside us. He is waiting on us to speak words of faith, so those seeds can reproduce what they're automatically ready, willing, and able to reproduce. The Word calls this faith that works. We have to activate faith with words. Amen?

Once again, we have to believe it and declare it so that we receive it. And we need to do this more and more. Dr. Craig Rench traveled with me for a season and taught this often. Let's capture his insight now. When we pray by faith and declare by faith, we need to start praising the Lord for His Word and thanking Him for answering His promises. If we have asked Him, and believe He hears us, and declare that we have received whatever we believed, we do not need to ask again. We thoroughly need to believe. We're not talking about intercession for someone else. We're describing a petition that we trust God for now. Either we believe He is going to give it to us in His time, or we don't know. Sincere, authentic, biblical faith in the Lord and the Word always believes, knows, and sees!

We covered Hebrews 10:23 in the previous chapter: we need to "hold firmly to the confession of our hope." And hope is substance, what our faith consists of. So, let's hold firmly to that substance! In other words, let's refuse to let go of what you're hoping for, of what we confess with our words, without wavering regardless of circumstances. "For He who promised is faithful." He gave us His Word, His promise, and He is faithful to fulfill His heart.

That was my final Scripture for this chapter. Now, I share a few life applications, some personal stories of grace by faith that works.

I was asked recently to go pray for a lady full of cancer and not expected to live beyond two weeks. I could see fear in her eyes. She had taught science her whole career. She knew how serious her condition was. I don't know exactly how to explain what her legs and arms looked like, perhaps like dwindling twigs or like drooping skin on shrinking bones.

When we walked in, her husband was talking about planning her funeral and other details. The mother-in-law appeared to be skeptical. The sister-in-law might have been a nurse. A couple of friends in the room kept asking, "Do you feel anything? Do you feel anything?" They wanted outward signs instead of believing the Word. I was discerning the world of fear, the scientific world, the funeral-planning world, the skeptic world, the medical world, and the carnal, we need-a-sign world. There were six different streams in the room.

They asked me to come to pray and I was thinking, "Okay, what am I supposed to do?" After they all agonized a little bit, I simply, quietly, briefly talked with the lady. Then I asked, "What do you want? I need to know what you want." And she said, "I want to live physically. I

# NOW FAITH!

want a miracle from God to destroy this cancer in my body so I can come back to life. I want to live physically."

I saw her faith and asked with hope and care, "Well, I can pray? I can agree with that because you believe." So, I started declaring the Word, confidently speaking the Word in the name of Jesus. The next day, we received news that she could think a little clearer. The next day, we heard that she was getting some strength back. I knew that every person in that room was a Christian. Every person in that room seemed to have faltering faith because each was tied to everything except the simple, powerful Word of God.

Do we see how easily the Church is now and will increasingly be deceived in these last days? When it all shakes down, the only hope and power that will remain is the Word of God. Let's ponder that. Amen? Everything else is going to come and go. The only thing that's going to remain is the Word. Are we tracking together? I want us to err on the side of the Word. Actually, I want us to declare the Word. So, we need to hold fast our confession.

If we are praying with a burden from the Lord in intercession, let's keep repeating our prayer with faith until God lifts the burden of intercession. This is God trusting us with His heart. This was a burden from the Lord, and He knows how and when to lift the burden. If we're asking God about things, let's keep asking.

Intercession normally expresses a different focus in prayer than petition. When we petition God by faith to heal or deliver, for example, we should pray it once. Let's be specific with God every time. Whether in intercession or petition, let's remember to speak by faith from our spirit "whatsoever things we desire." Jesus did not place a limit on passion.

We opened this chapter with corresponding acts of faith, so let's end with a couple of other examples. A mechanic working on our car might say, "I think this is good enough," and then put the carburetor back on. As a result, it is highly unlikely our car is going to run well for long. No matter how good the mechanic thinks our car is going to be, he needs to finish the action required for during his best, not merely good enough.

Similarly, I remember preaching then ministering when a man came forward for me pray for his eyes. When I finished, he took his glasses off and stomped on them right in front of the altar. His eyes were not healed that night. Stomping on glasses is not a corresponding act of faith. That might be a corresponding act of something else because he went home that night driving legally blind. I don't think God wants us to presume, then do stuff that's illegal.

Another weekend, after I had proclaimed the Word, someone asked, "Am I not living in faith by taking medicine my doctor prescribed?"

I replied with truth in love, "Your medicine has nothing to do with your faith. What's your medicine do?" That person said, "Well, it's keeping my sugar down." I replied, "Well, if it's keeping you alive, now you have time for your faith to grow. If you're dead, there's no more chance for your faith to grow." In other words, friends, if insulin is helping to maintain a healthy blood sugar level, then taking essential meds is not a lack of faith. It's giving more time for faith to grow. We need to have wisdom in our acts of faith.

Before harvest time, seed starts with a bud and then a stalk, then a mature grain. It grows incrementally. Our faith in action should grow as the seed, producing step by step, one day at a time. That's why God gave us a brain.

Some people ask me, "What about you and your story?" The Lord has been teaching me for more many years to grow in grace by faith, in His Word and Spirit. The Lord did not and is not presently growing

# NOW FAITH!

my faith overnight. God speaks to me in His timing. In His time, my faith grows so I can believe and receive what God is saying and doing in that time. Each of us is on a different rung on the ladder of faith.

When I was in Terre Haute, Indiana and after I proclaimed the Word, a lady came forward as I started to minister faith and love, healing, and hope. She said she was blind, and she used a white cane, moving it side to side to know where to walk. When I asked what she wanted, she said, "I want my vision…I want to see." I don't remember particularly feeling any super faith. I gently placed my hands on her eyes and declared, "Lord, let her eyes open now in Jesus' name." Then, she looked at me and nothing apparently changed.

That Sunday evening, I arrived early for a 5:00 pm gathering. It didn't get dark until about nine o'clock at night, so sunlight was still bright. I noticed immediately that the lady who was blind was working out in the flower bed in front of the worship center, pulling weeds and pruning flowers. I asked, "Are you the lady that was blind this morning?" She nearly shouted with joy, "Yes, but I can see." I asked again, "Well, how did it happen?" She explained, "I went home and took a nap. When I woke up, I could see!"

And the Kingdom of God is like a man who sows seeds. Then, he goes to bed. When he wakes up, he doesn't know how it works. Come on! I still get goosebumps all over my body thinking about the seed of God's Word. God's seed did that. Let's agree with Him to do that.

When I was preaching and ministering in another city, Michael Perkins came. He's a close evangelist friend into whose ministry we have sown some seed. He had eye problems and had worn glasses for a decade. By faith in the Word and Spirit, I was releasing words of knowledge. Suddenly, Michael took off his glasses. He could see perfectly. Now, listen to this: nobody laid hands on him. Nobody spoke a word to him. But through the words the Holy Spirit in me was releasing into the atmosphere, Michael's faith was so strong that those words could take root in his spirit garden and produce that amazing harvest almost instantaneously!

I will tell you a lot more stories about faith in the rest of this book and future messages. Most of the time, I've seen the greatest extraordinary miracles when I didn't know how it was even possible. I simply stood by faith on the Word. Then, other times when I thought, "Oh, I know something's going happen, nothing ever happened. We might think we would experience the opposite of that. But when faith in God is working, He sometimes intends for it to work when our flesh is the weakest, and our spirits are soaring. Do you agree? So, I want to challenge us to lose ourselves again in faith, believing that if we'll say what God's Word says, it will happen. He cannot lie. Amen? In Jesus' name, Amen!

# 9
# CORRESPONDING ACTIONS WITH OUR FAITH

In this chapter, we will focus on more corresponding actions or acts of faith that help our faith grow. That's the truth we explore here with now faith. We recall that our daughter-in-law Megan invited our whole family for a spaghetti dinner. While she finished cooking the pasta, I'll never forget her words that marked my heart. She asked our little granddaughter, Kaylee Claire, to take a string of the spaghetti and throw it on the wall. And my daughter-in-law said, "If it sticks, it's ready." And it stuck, so we could enjoy the spaghetti. Let's pray truth sticks here now.

I am motivated to teach many distinct, different angles of faith. As I offer multiple angles, I believe at least one will stick. Then, we'll be able to operate in the faith. Right? I want us to operate in faith based on what Scripture says and not what the world or circumstances say.

In James 2:14-22, the brother of Jesus wrote, "What use is it, my brothers and sisters, if someone says he has faith, but he has no works? Can that faith save him? If a brother or a sister is without clothing and in need of daily food and one of you says, 'Go in peace be warmed and be filled', yet you do not give what is necessary for their body, what use is that? In the same way, faith also, if it has no works, is dead, being by itself. But if someone may well say, 'You have faith and I have works' then show me your faith without the works and I will show you my faith by my works. Do you believe that? God is one, you do well. The demons also believe and shudder. But are you willing to acknowledge, you foolish person, that faith without works is useless? Was our father Abraham not justified by works when he offered up his son Isaac on the altar? You see that faith was working with his works, and as a result of the works, faith was perfected."

Let's pray. Now, Father, I trust you to help us learn to receive your Word that's implanted in our hearts so that it produces the harvest it was sent to produce. In Jesus' name I pray. Amen.

Now let's explore what Jesus taught in Mark 4:26 as an anchor passage for this chapter, "The kingdom of God is like a man who cast seed upon the soil. And he goes to bed at night, and he gets up daily. And the seed sprouts and grows, he himself does not know. The soil produces crops by itself: first the stalk, then the head, then the mature grain in the head. Now, when the crop permits, he immediately puts in the sickle because the harvest has come."

Friends, sometimes our attempts to perform corresponding acts of faith or actions of faith accomplish little or nothing at all. I propose that the greatest act of faith is doing what the Word says, and then going to bed at night. Sometimes we attempt things we call acts of faith that are rote or repetitious, because we really don't believe what the Word says. Perhaps the greatest evidence of believing the Word is resting in the reality of the Word, and resting in its intended purpose, the real reason for which it was sent. It accomplishes little or no good to attempt something in our flesh or with wrong motives. Let's consider an analogy.

Our acts of faith need to be in alignment with our development of faith. A familiar story in Matthew 14 is an example of this principle. Peter and the disciples were caught on the Sea of Galilee in a small fishing boat during a raging storm. They saw Jesus, walking on the water, but thought he was a ghost, and they were afraid. Jesus said, "Don't be afraid, it's Me." Then Peter said to Jesus, "If it's You, Lord, call me to You." Well, obviously Peter's faith had not yet developed to the same level as Jesus. The Messiah had faith to walk on water without sinking, regardless of how rough or turbulent the wind and waves, life's circumstances. Clearly, Peter had not matured in his faith to that depth. He was beyond his heart and over his head in water.

Have you ever wondered why Jesus would call Peter into a situation where He knew Peter would fail? When I asked Jesus that question, He referred me to the Scriptures. Through the Word, I sensed Jesus say, "I did not force Peter into that situation. Peter pressed me, so I tested his faith." At first, I did not understand what Jesus meant. But I finally noted that Peter said, "If it's You, Lord, call me to You." So, Jesus could not lie. He is Lord and cannot lie.

Sometimes if we're naïve and we presume that because another person experienced a miracle, then we could receive it also. However, we don't know how that other person who experienced a miracle needed to grow to develop faith in order to see the miracle manifest. We don't know the back story of people. We might hear part of their testimonies, but we don't know what they've done in the secret place behind closed doors with their Heavenly Father. So, when we see what they're receiving, we don't know the journey of faith they have traveled.

Perhaps Peter put Jesus in an awkward position because the Savior could not lie by saying, "No, it's not me. Don't come out here because you're going to sink." He had to be honest. So, Jesus invited Peter, "Come." One word! Remember, "Faith comes by hearing and hearing by the Word of God." One word from Jesus gave Peter enough power to walk on storms temporarily. What happened to Peter in the tempestuous storm? Because Peter's faith was not adequately developed, he took his eyes off the Source of perfecting faith and focused on distracting sources of fear and unbelief. And he sank.

This is our daily journey: the necessity of doing what it takes to develop our faith. Do you agree with that principle? Note Matthew 14:28 where Peter quickly became preoccupied with the circumstances, the challenges, and he lost faith. Now, circumstances are a reality. They're real. We should not deny circumstances. But we should always acknowledge that there is a greater reality. That is the eternal reality that God's Word cannot lie. Temporary circumstances come and go. We need to learn how by faith we can grasp eternal realities. If we follow truth, it always leads us to the Person Jesus Christ. If we follow circumstances, we will always need to endure more challenges. We need to choose to follow truth. Amen?

A lot of people have tried to teach on healing, on faith, or on authority. Many have actually given these a bad name. God waits for us to develop our soil so that the crop can produce what He intends, but God cannot remove thorns, rocks, and hardpack soil. That's the corresponding action we need to implement. God's seed is always good, but it's up to us to prepare the soil so the seed can do in us what the Lord intends.

So, I want to write more about receiving healing because some people aren't developed in their faith. I've heard healing preachers say, "Well, stop taking your medicine or don't consult your doctor because those actions lack faith." Should any person ever tell anyone not to consult a doctor or not to take medicine that doctor prescribed?

For example, a person comes forward for prayer, but extreme pain incapacitates that person's adequate faith and focus so he or she cannot think. For that person, a prayer for healing becomes merely noisy, reverberating, overblown, inflammatory prayer. You know

## NOW FAITH!

how severe pain debilitates. That person took a pill to control pain, comes forward for prayer, hopes for a healing manifestation, but the pain doesn't leave. Then that person might decide, "I'm going to stop taking that pill because it's a lack of faith."

If God didn't tell him or her to do that, then we should avoid speaking for God or wait until that person's faith is adequate to believe and receive God's voice. If a pill keeps the pain level down so that person can focus on Scripture, that pill might be helping to heal. A pill for pain will not keep them from being healed. If a pill can suppress pain so faith can develop, then we should allow for faith to develop until that person can receive healing. Then, when healing manifests, the harvest can be a full crop. Do we understand and agree?

We need the mind of Messiah (Christ) and we need to agree with our own mind fully engaged. These are not in opposition to each other. I don't want you to take this wrong. Jesus never told anybody to go take a bottle of pills, not one time in His ministry. Neither am I suggesting we do that. Here is what I am saying: if our pain has increased to the level of clear necessity for an occasional pill, let's keep taking it until our faith grows. Then, God's Word can produce healing and we will no longer need an occasional pill. Again, we need to grow faith right where we live in pain. Does that make sense?

We cannot start where Benny Hinn, Oral Roberts, Bill Johnson, Todd White, or someone else is gifted or has grown. We have to start with where we are in faith development. We should not press people into corners when they don't have faith. That would be like calling people out of a boat during a storm when they haven't learned to walk on water. Come on!

We need to teach people how to live by faith in the Word of the Lord and to develop their faith. And we need to help people where they are. We should never tell anyone to take away their medication, because they need first to learn their confession and profession. Our confession is a process, growing our faith is a process, intimacy with Jesus is a process, growing in our authority is a process, and it all takes time. It's seed time and harvest, seed time and harvest.

This is really practical, but we need to teach it, receive it, believe it, and practice it. We need to plant the right amount of seed to produce the harvest we desire. So, confessing the Word and declaring the Word is a Joshua 1:8 reality: we never let the Word of God depart from our mouth. We meditate on it day and night. We do what it says. Corresponding acts of faith are doing what the Word says, not what our emotions shout.

Let's repeat that aloud now: corresponding acts of faith are doing what the Word of God says, not what our emotions shout. What does He say? Let's search for a Bible passage that deals with what we need, then do what the Words says. And let's be slow to do what people say, unless they counsel from the Word and in the spirit of Jesus. Let's do what the Word says.

When I was ministering in the Bronx Bethany congregation in New York, I was preaching during a weekend meeting with about 600 Jamaicans. It was an interesting gathering during my first weekend there. I returned there for various weekend awakening encounters during the next three years. This first time, the pastor invited me to preach and minister Friday night, Saturday morning, Saturday night, and Sunday morning. After we finished Friday night, I went back to my hotel and sensed the Lord saying, "I want you to lead them in public confession tomorrow morning." I replied, "Well, that's not what they asked me to do." And the Lord persisted, "I want you to lead them in public confession tomorrow morning." When I arrived, they led an hour of worship, then I declared, "We're going to confess sins so the Lord will forgive us. Then, we can pray for each other, and we can be healed."

# NOW FAITH!

From about 10:00 am until 8:00 pm, they never stopped standing in line at the microphone to confess. Person after person took a total of 10 hours. One would finish and one or two others were already standing in line to confess. There was always someone standing in line. They kept getting rid of things that were blocking God from being able to move. People of all ages, old and young, kept confessing sins such as: "I had an abortion when I was age 13." Similar depth of need was being confessed over and over, person after person. I didn't know when they were going to finish. We were supposed to have morning and evening meetings, but they lasted from 10:00 am until 8:00 pm. Finally, nobody needed to confess anything else.

We all knew what the Lord did on Saturday: He removed weeds, rocks, hardness, and thorns. When the congregation gathered on Sunday morning, I didn't know what to expect. Now, when we received the Word of the Lord that Sunday morning, the soil of their hearts was ready to produce a harvest automatically. And that harvest continued to be produced from 9:00 am until 5:30 pm that evening. I prayed a short, simple prayer of faith near what I thought would be the end of the meeting. Then, the Lord healed 400 persons before we finished. Now, listen: we need to hear this. The altar was lined with medicine and prescriptions. I didn't even mention medicine. The entire altar was lined with medicine. Person after person declared, "I don't need this any longer!" We experienced the genius miracle of how God did this!

The Holy Spirit's process during 10 hours on Saturday to break up the soil had prepared right hearts and right faith. This illustrates a great correlation with how long it takes us to align and develop our faith with the Word. Then, we can live in the manifestation of what the Word intends to produce and has God's power to produce. We can spread growth in the Word and faith over months or we can grow in a 10-hour day. How or how long we come to faith is not so important. The Lord will accomplish what we believe and receive. He is faithful and can't lie.

I ministered at Flint Central Church of the Nazarene when Dr. Glen Gardner was the pastor. During one altar call, the Lord restored hearing to a deaf boy and healed a lame man who walked out of his wheelchair. The Spirit of God poured out a lot of miracles! A banker was healed of fear. A lady placed her depression medication on the altar, and declared, "God just healed me from depression." I asked, "How do you know?" She replied, "I really know." I had not even laid my hands on her. That was many years ago and that lady has been a partner supporting our ministry ever since. That depression has never plagued her again.

Everyone is at a different level in faith development. We should never generalize by saying, "Well, if you had faith, you could do this." That's not our responsibility. We faithfully release seeds of truth to kingdoms like a person who's sow seeds. Some of the soil is good or receptive. Some of the soil is bad or resistant.

Have we learned the genius of Jesus teaching in parables? He never explained these to His followers unless He was in secret or privacy with them. He told parables so listeners who needed to understand and discover the truth themselves. That's the genius of His teaching with parables. The disciples came to Him later and asked, "What is the meaning?" Jesus responded, "To those outside of faith I speak in parables, but to you with faith I have given the secrets of the Kingdom."

Let's learn more about Jesus and His approach together. A parable puts the burden on us to dig out the truth, which is the genius of God. In other words, we have to do the work to get our soil ready, so that our faith is developing. Do you get it? And parables are like mysteries that reveal truth. For example, here's a parable. Don't try

# NOW FAITH!

to obtain a coat made of bear fur while the bear is still alive. That's a parable. We can figure out the truth behind that parable easily, right? But that's a parable.

Now, an illustration explains a parable. Do we understand why people like illustrations in American preaching so much? Because they don't have to get their soil ready. They're reaping off someone else's revelation. While a few persons invest time in the secret place of the Word and faith, preparing the soil, most people like illustrations and stories. Jesus did not want to give people shortcuts, so He taught in parables, causing the crowds to go home thinking what He taught made no sense, but they knew they heard truth and needed to start digging. We serve listeners more effectively when we bombard them with enough seeds of truth that they know it is true. But they must still search for the deeper meaning. That's what makes our faith develop and the faith of others grow also. Are we receiving and believing this?

Here are some additional principles toward activating faith. We need to agree with the Spirit to empower our faith on the front end, before we get sick, instead of waiting until a doctor says there's no hope. It's better, easier, and less expensive to develop our faith before we need it than to wait until only a miracle from God is our answer. Then, we're always trying to play catch up. Let's live to confess the Word. Let's live to meditate on the Word. Let's live to believe the Word prior to a catastrophe. Then, we will be much more equipped to rise above all the adversity that the world, the flesh, and the devil will bring against the Word of God and us.

People inform me every day that their doctor said there's no hope. Sometimes, they hope my development of faith can help their deficiency of faith. But they waited until they were desperate before they reached out toward someone with faith. Do you experience this also? Now, succinctly, clearly, with no apologies, remember that medicine cannot cure you and it cannot keep you from being cured. While we should not feel guilty about occasional need for medication, we should avoid dependence on it. If medication provides us time to develop our faith, we should not feel condemned for the need to use it. Again, medication might give us time to develop our faith.

In Luke 17, we find the story of the ten lepers and another example of corresponding action for our faith. Let's begin with Luke 17:11, "While Jesus was on the way to Jerusalem, He was passing between Samaria and Galilee. And as He entered a village ten men with leprosy who stood at a distance met Him. And they raised their voices saying, 'Jesus, Master, have mercy on us.' When He saw them, He said to them, 'Go and show yourself to the priest. As they were going, they were cleansed.'"

What was their corresponding act of faith? They did what He told them to do. He instructed, "Go to the priest" and they went to the priest. Their faith was developed adequately, so that the words Jesus gave them could manifest in their physical bodies when they did what He instructed them to do. Do you see their corresponding act of faith? Jesus is always the answer to our needs and questions. And He is always the answer for how our faith is developed. Faith comes by hearing and obeying the Word of God. Amen?

This was an example of a parallel truth in Psalm 107:20, "He sent His word to them, and healed them" as they obeyed His words. Jesus sent His Word to them and healed them. They did what His words said for them to do: a corresponding act of faith. Sometimes praying all night is not an act of faith. Instead, it could be an act of worry. If the Lord does not tell us to pray all night, then praying all night is not an act of faith. Sometimes we demonstrate a greater act of faith by going to sleep, trusting God's Word and His work.

Other times, praying all night can be an act of faith, but not normally when we're believing for something specifically for ourselves.

# NOW FAITH!

Perhaps we have a burden of intercession of His Spirit pouring through us for a city, a family, a situation in a government. That burden could be the Holy Spirit accessing our spirit, soul, and body as an intercession chamber. And as long as He wants to pray, let Him go for it. Come on!

However, when we're believing for something, it is not always faith to keep repeating it over and over and over again. A couple of years ago, the Lord interrupted my study time in the Word and prayer with His question, "Why do you take your medication?" I responded, "Because I am sick." About 10 minutes later, He asked me again, "Why do you take your medicine?" That time I answered, "Because my doctor is a Christian and he told me I needed it." I told Jesus my doctor was a Christian because I thought that would impress the Lord. However, about 10 minutes later, Jesus asked a third time, "Why do you take your medicine?" I repeated, "Because I believe I am sick." Then His response to me was, "Why don't you believe you are well?"

I live about half of each day listening to the Word, studying the Word, and meditating on the Word. So, my faith is probably in a little different place than somebody who has heard very little or nothing from the Lord or the Word. Okay? When God repeated that question three times, I finally thought, "Well, if Jesus says I need to trust and believe His Word that I am well, then He doesn't really think I need the medicine." But I still needed to trust His Spirit and believe His Word, then act in faith by not taking my medicine. It was essential that my conscience was clear because faith works with a clear conscience. If our conscience isn't clear, we cannot respond with sincere faith.

We should not expect someone to live by grace through faith like anyone else does. We are not the judge of the conscience. The Lord through His Word and Spirit is the judge of the conscience. I thought, "My conscience is clear. Then, I need to believe in what Jesus just spoke to me. I need to quit depending on my own understanding and my medication." I did and He healed my body of five issues. When I activated the gift of faith the Lord gave me, then demonstrated a corresponding action, I was healed. My act of faith was to stop taking the medicine. However, remember that another person might need a clear conscience in order to continue taking medicine.

Here is another example. In 2014, I was preaching and ministering in a revival in Tennessee. God gave me a dream at 2:00 very early one morning that I was supposed to provide funding for Dr. Daniel and Carol Ketchum to move to Jerusalem, Israel. God gave me a dream. I did not know how I was going to help support them financially. I only clearly knew God gave me a dream. So, I prayed about it at 2:00 am, then I went back to sleep. When I woke up, I thought "That's weird." So, I called Daniel and told him the dream. He responded, "Well, it resounds and resonates in my heart. Carol and I will pray." Then, a few weeks later, they resigned from the Global Ministry Center and moved to Jerusalem. My act of faith was being obedient to the dream the Lord gave me. I knew it was His voice.

So, please hear my heart. I did not know how details would come together for the Ketchum's financial support. My act of faith was to hear God's Word and commit to support this couple called by God, ready and willing to minister in Israel. This did not come from me: I had no awareness about Daniel and Carol Ketchum were already praying about ministering in Israel. So, the guidance and faith did not come from Dan Bohi's emotions. That was clearly a dream from God. He gave me adequate faith and obedience to know that when He wants me to do something, He will provide the miracle. My act of faith was, "Lord, I trust You to enable giving to increase in this ministry." The act of faith came prior to the increase of revenue. The Lord, the Spirit, and the Word were teaching me how to develop my faith. Are you hearing me?

Then, a couple of years later, God challenged me to invite Dr. Craig Rench to join our team as an intercessor. Again, I thought, "How in

# NOW FAITH!

the world am I going to fund him also?" You might not realize that most itinerate evangelists do not make enough money to even pay themselves, let alone support somebody else. But that's just the way the Lord is. He and many of you had been helping our ministry to support Daniel and Carol in Israel. Next, God was saying to me, "Ask Craig Rench to come with you and support him also." The Lord was telling me to do that.

I was thinking, "Okay, it worked the first time, but I don't know. God, is this You or me?" So, I was questioning. For faith to develop, we have to ponder some natural questions that only the Word of God can answer supernaturally. If faith is a muscle, we need to exercise it. Are we getting this? I couldn't simply say, "Well, my faith is needing to grow." I needed to apply acts of faith for my faith to grow. In other words, we need to develop to the point that we rely on God alone. We cannot rely on ourselves. Self-reliance is not faith. Leaning on our own thoughts and resources is merely a little human ingenuity, a little charisma, a little talent, and a little ability.

I asked the Lord and He answered, "I am the Lord, Dan. This is Me." So, I had a clear assurance and conscience. I called Craig, told him what I sensed from the Lord and the Word, and invited him to join our team. He said, "Well, I haven't heard anything from God." I said, "I think you've heard; you're just not listening." I had never said that to anybody in my life. I've never said that to anybody since then. But the Lord told me to assure Craig that the Lord was talking to him. "But, Craig, you're not listening."

Craig replied honestly, "No one has ever accused me of that before. I listen to God all day long." When Craig hung up the phone, he went to his prayer chair, sat down for 15 minutes, and the Lord spoke to him, "Craig, I've been trying to tell you this for months, but you're not listening." So, Craig called me back immediately and said, "Okay,

I'm going to minister with you," and he resigned from the church he pastored.

Now listen to this. As soon as Craig started ministering and teaching intercession with me, my two biggest donors could no longer give money. I had nothing but worry and fear the first month, because I wondered, "Have I made the biggest mistake of my life? This brother who was receiving a secure salary, retirement plan, and security, is now going to travel with me, but my generous giving partners whom I thought were secure, were no longer giving." So, I felt worry, which made me go back to the Word. Are you hearing what I'm teaching?

So, by the time we got to the end of that first year that Craig was with me, we had lost two major donors. But by the end of the year, our partner giving was up 20% over the previous year. The only way we knew how to explain it was that we kept trusting God and our act of faith was to do what God said to do. When He gave us faith, His manifestation of provision and prosperity had a place to deposit what we needed. My faith needed to be developed.

Brothers and sisters, we cannot develop each other's faith. Only we ourselves can use common sense, make our soil good, develop our faith, and plant some good seed. We cannot normally discern a full corresponding act of faith until we know that the full manifestation is right around the corner. And only our clear conscience can produce sincere faith.

If we're sick, we should not deny we're sick; don't lie. But we should deny the right for sickness to remain in us. How and why? Because we are the temple of the Holy Spirit. We're the dwelling place of God, we're the outpost of the kingdom of God, we're covered by the blood, and we're redeemed by the sacrifice of Jesus.

So, sickness doesn't have a right to remain in us. We need to deny the right for adversity to happen, but we cannot deny the fact that it's real, it's hard, it hits us often and increasingly as the "love of most grows cold." So, that's why we need to cooperate with the Lord to develop our faith. Are you with me?

We must not say all the right things mixed with fear, because that actually makes our hearts harder. I've heard people declaring Scripture about healing, or Scripture about prosperity, or Scripture about reconciliation versus restoration. For many, it's like a mantra, like a root routine, but it has nothing to do with faith. Instead, many of their statements have everything to do with masking an inward fear that only trusting the Word of God can remove. He doesn't need our repetitious words. He needs our heart to believe so we can rest.

This is a little harder lesson, isn't it brothers and sisters? We should not say all the right things in fear. Sometimes the greatest corresponding act of faith is taking a nap or going to bed at night or finding another way to relax so the Lord can restore sincere shalom. God called us to this, so let's believe and receive.

Let's close this chapter with two stories starting in John 4:47, "When he heard that Jesus had come from Judea into Galilee, he went to him and began asking him to come down and heal his son for he was at the point of death. Then, Jesus said to him, 'Unless you people see signs and wonders, you simply will not believe.'" Now that's interesting! Jesus calls out people who are always seeking for outward signs before they believe. He doesn't want people to need fleshly proof. He doesn't like it. This is what the man said to Jesus in response, "Sir, come down before my child dies." In other words, the man didn't get offended at Jesus's response.

Now, let's listen carefully, remembering that Jesus' Word is what gives us faith. Right? Jesus said to him, "Go, your son is alive. And the man believed the word that Jesus spoke to him." Jesus didn't give him a sign or a wonder. He didn't do anything visible right there. The man simply believed the word that Jesus spoke to him. "And as he was now going down, his servants met him, saying that his son was alive. So, he inquired of them the hour when he began to get better." So, this wasn't an instant healing. Rather, his son "began to get better."

The servants said to him, "Yesterday, at the seventh hour the fever left." So, the father knew that it was at that same hour Jesus said to him, 'Your son is alive.' And he himself became a believer and his whole household." I love that story! What was the father's act of faith? Going home. He simply did what Jesus said. Jesus said, "Go home. Your son is going to be okay." And the man believed Jesus' words. Whoa, I want to believe Jesus' Word like that, don't you? I don't want to wait until I feel something or see something or hear something. I want to hear His Word and believe that reality. Amen?

Our final story is in John 5:47, "But if you don't believe his writings, how will you believe my words?" Let's pause here. If we can't believe what's written in the Bible, we'll never believe when the Spirit speaks to our spirit. Faith starts by believing the written word. We need to believe what is written so we can start believing what is spoken.

Then, let's turn to John 6:1: "Now after these things, Jesus went away to the other side of the Sea of Galilee, to Tiberius, and a large crowd was following him because they were watching the signs that he was performing on those who were sick. But Jesus went up on the mountain. There he sat with his disciples." Sometimes the best response to a large crowd coming to you for miracles, is to find a small group of people who believe, sit still, and rest.

What is the takeaway from this chapter? Our faith must be developed by us. Our soil must be prepared by us. The only way this really happens is for us to learn, really learn to trust and believe what God's Word says.

## NOW FAITH!

There are no shortcuts. We can go to conferences, seminars, anointed people, and feel something good. But 90% of the time, that feeling doesn't last.

Or we can do the hard work of getting our soil ready, building ourselves up in the most holy faith, and believing what God's Word says. Then, we can walk in a harvest of hope, healing, holiness, anointing, authority, intimacy, compassion, and prosperity in spirit, soul, and body. Because God's Word is true, and He cannot lie.

NOW FAITH!

# 10

## OVERFLOWING WITH HOPE

In this chapter, we will feature another way of understanding and living by faith. First, let's remember what motivated these 12 messages and chapters on faith. Medical doctor Luke recorded a key question in Luke 18:8 when Jesus asked, "When I come back to the earth, will I even find faith?" Let's agree again: we want to be among those in whom He finds faith. Right? We want to be living by grace through faith. We will not settle for living religion or routine.

Instead, we want to be living from the perspective of what the Word of God says and not by every other word. Our goal is to be found faithful when Jesus returns. Amen? That is the motivation behind this entire series. Why are we studying many unique ways of understanding and living by faith? So that each of us will retain at least one of these Scriptures and one of these principles.

I keep reviewing a story about my daughter-in-law who hosted our whole family for a spaghetti dinner. She let our granddaughter grab one of the spaghetti strands and throw it on the wall. She said, "When it sticks on the wall, it's ready to eat."

Again, I am hoping that at least one of these Scriptures, one of these principles will stick. Then, we'll start living the faith and we'll start reproducing the life and ministry of Jesus as normal lifestyle. This chapter will focus on faith overflowing with hope. We possess and practice faith only if we experience hope.

Let's return to Hebrews 11:1 and dive into the Word of the Lord: "Faith is the substance of things hoped for and the evidence or proof of things not seen." Faith is the substance and essence of what we're hoping for. So, what are we hoping for? Is our faith overflowing with hope? Does our faith exhibit any substance? Those are questions we hope to answer now.

If we don't hope for, long for, or desire anything specific, our faith has little or no substance. Hebrews 11:6 reminds us, "Without faith, it's impossible to please Him. For the one who comes to God must believe that He exists and that He proves to be the one who awards those who seek Him." While we believe the Lord exists, we can't prove or explain Him. He is revealed to us by the Spirit and the Word. We can't prove Him or explain Him to any person or group, but He can reveal Himself to anyone. By His revelation, we must believe that He exists. He proves that He is God by rewarding those who seek Him. Amen?

How does God prove to us or anyone, anytime, anywhere that He is God? By rewarding us when we seek Him in faith. Do we think God demonstrates more effective and efficient ways to reward us than other persons could? Yes: there's no competition! I think God's reward system and motivation to bless us is off the charts!

Let's learn together from a sequence of several Scriptures why we should have faith and why we should have hope. 2 Peter 1:3 teaches, "For His divine power has granted to us everything pertaining to life and godliness, through the true knowledge of Him who called us by His own glory and excellence." Everything we need for physical life and eternal life is in our spirit. Everything we need for life here on earth, as well as life here on the new earth, has already been

## NOW FAITH!

deposited into our spirit. Everything we'll need for eternity has been given to us when we're born again. And we know that only through the true knowledge of Him.

Another verse supporting this principle is Philemon 1:6, "If you want your faith to become effective and the fellowship of your faith to become effective, it's only effective in the acknowledgment of what you have in Christ Jesus." We need to start informing our hearts that what we have in Christ is effective! We start to plant these seeds in the soil of our hearts with audible, verbal statements of faith, because that's what the Word of God says is ours. Do you really believe that now? Whatever the Word says is what Christ says, because Christ is the Word made flesh. Every word of His is Spirit-breathed. The Holy Spirit brings the Word to life.

Everything the Word of God says is ours, and that is what we should be saying to ourselves because it is ours! That practice builds our faith so we're willing and able to hope for more! The more begins here: we realize God has already given us all we need in our spirit by His Spirit.

Romans 5:1-5 are the favorite five verses of the chairman of our ministry board because Paul describes hope as part of the substance of faith, what we believe for. "Therefore, having been justified by faith, we have peace with God, through our Lord Jesus Christ, through whom we also have obtained our introduction by faith into this grace in which we stand." Let's pause there a moment. We realize we are justified and born again by faith. The Lord also brings us into and empowers us to remain in a deeper grace, which we believe is sanctifying grace. While I cannot develop that theme further now, know this: I believe, I practice, and I teach many principles on holy hearts and holy lives or entire sanctification. Faith enables us to be justified. Faith also enables us to be sanctified so we can stand steadfast and valiant in victory.

Let's continue in Romans 5:2, "And we celebrate in hope of the glory of God." Now, this is amazing. Here are simple steps from the Word that each of us needs to take: we're born again so that we can be led into entire sanctification. Then, our hope can be set free to soar within the glory that's now within us!

Paul teaches an important principle in 2 Thessalonians 2:13. We should all give thanks all the time, because God has chosen all of us for salvation through the sanctifying work of the Spirit and belief in the truth, so that He can put His glory in us. His glory is any attribute that only Jesus or God can manifest in and through us.

His glory is His manifested attribute, which includes peace in forgiveness and cleansing and fulness, healing, deliverance, reconciliation, restoration, redemption, provision, and much more. Glory is His manifested attribute that only God's glory and power can pour into us and through us for our marriage, family, congregation, work colleagues, neighbors, and others. When, not if, but when we allow God to justify and sanctify us by faith, He overflows in our heart and home a huge opportunity to start dreaming about all that's wrapped up in the glory that He has put inside us! Right?

Additionally, as we note in Romans 5:3, "We also celebrate in our tribulations." When we realize what the Spirit has actually and already poured into us, then instead of trying to fight tribulations, now we celebrate them. We thank God for tribulations, sufferings! Why? Because the Word of God teaches us that trials, testing, trauma, torments, terror, and temptations will produce perseverance, which is the number one quality we in the end-time Bride of Christ truly need. We overcome by the blood of Jesus the Lamb and overflow by faith with hope.

If we learn to celebrate in the contradiction of what the Word says is ours, the Spirit enables our perseverance to grow. Come on! Then,

# NOW FAITH!

"perseverance produces character", and changes the way we are. Then, "character produces hope. And hope does not disappoint us, because it's the love of God that's been poured within our hearts through the Holy Spirit who was given to us."

Yes! That's so good; let's pause and reflect again. When we attain hope that does not disappoint us, we will be living by faith constantly, rather than living by fear, doubt, discouragement, and unbelief. So, hope is necessary for faith to exist. Do we agree?

Now, let's turn one page in our Bibles to Romans 4:18, "In hope against hope, Abraham believed so that he might become a father of many nations according to what had been spoken, 'So shall your descendants be.'"

Oh, friend, when there's no hope in the natural, then the Spirit is able to usher us into the supernatural. What is the supernatural? A manifestation attributed to some "force" beyond scientific understanding or the laws of nature. In other words, the supernatural from the LORD God is the realm of the Holy Spirit. How can we enter the supernatural? By the Holy Spirit through the Word of God. Come on!

We're learning how faith overflows in hope. Hope needs faith, seeks faith, and believes for more faith. This becomes personal for each of us, doesn't it? It is personal for me. My doctors tell me there is no hope for my left hip to recover without hip replacement surgery. I believe my left hip would be easier for God to heal than to produce a child at age 100 like He did for Abraham and Sarah.

How do I keep believing? By the Spirit through the Word, and in miracle after miracle that I watch the Lord perform. In one congregation in California, I recently witnessed a lady with multiple sclerosis (MS) who had fallen, shattered her pelvis, and lived in terrible pain.

She could not stand up before she fell. After we prayed by faith with hope, she stood up and testified that the pain was gone.

Now faith can be garnered from what the Word says, rather than from what the world says. The Word gives faith a substance that is the power of God, what He eagerly waits to do in us. That's what the Bible calls "the glory!" Jesus told His disciples that if they believed what they hoped for, they would see the glory of God. (John 11:40). Does that bless you like it blesses me? Come on!

We know we cannot find hope in the world, so we go to the Word of God. Even before we fail to find hope in others, we remain in the Word of God. As we read, study, and apply the Word of God to our daily challenges and needs, we receive hope from the Lord of the Word. Hope! Let's see it and say it this way: hope is our goal setter. Hope is our goal setter. What we hope for sets a goal for what God eventually, actually enables us to achieve. Without setting a goal, there is little hope we will ever achieve anything significant. Faith overflows in hope.

In Colossians 1:27, we discover and remember, "This is the mystery that has been revealed to all the Gentiles. That is this: Christ in you the hope of glory." Again, the reality and the substance of faith is in us because what we're hoping for is already in us. The Lord placed hope into our hearts. Our hope will produce a faith that lets Him provide what only He can do in and through us. That's His glory being revealed. The reality is Christ. The Messiah is already in us. Everything we need for life and godliness. He is already in us. That's our reality! The hope is: we will stay in hope long enough for it to produce faith so that Jesus can start providing what only Christ can do in and through us.

"Faith is the substance of things hoped for." Now listen carefully: we should not try to exercise faith where hope should function already.

# NOW FAITH!

And we should not try to exercise hope where faith should function. Remember Romans 10:17, "Faith comes by hearing, and hearing by the words of Christ" or the Word of God. So, when we receive faith, it is because what we're hearing in the Word is what we begin to hope for. We should not get these in wrong order.

In other words, when the Word teaches, "By his stripes we were healed," then we hope that healing and health can become our reality: that we can be healed. In fact, we want healing to be our reality. Then, that is what we are expecting and what we're believing for. And that's when faith has a substance to hold on to and embrace. This is very specific.

I am preaching to myself right now. I typically preach to everybody else. But sometimes, I allow pain, disappointment, or delay to create a loud narrative in my own mind that releases words totally opposite of what the Word of God says. Please be honest with yourself and me if that's what you do also. When we face delays, distractions, and pain while we're praying, we sometimes start saying things that are contrary to what the Word of God says. And that's the dilemma of our fight of faith.

Do we comprehend one of the secrets of the Apostle Paul? I have not found in letters he wrote anything contrary to what the Spirit was saying to him. In other words, he didn't speak emotions. He didn't speak disappointments. He didn't speak fear. He didn't speak unbelief. He chose to speak and write only what the Lord said to him. And he was a human being like us.

Righteousness (right relationship with God and others) is revealed through the power of our words, which are initiated by the Spirit, which releases the glory, which allows God to do what only God can do. And that's on us. In other words, we should not ask, "Well, God, why don't you do in me what you did in Paul?" God can produce in us anything that we are willing to believe enough to declare audibly, simply, and clearly with faith. On the other hand, God cannot produce something in us that we are unwilling to believe enough to articulate at all.

The universe is formed by the Word of His power and held in place by the Word of His power. Nothing came into being beyond, "In the beginning was the Word." Our words, spoken in faith that overflows with hope, are vital, essential, essential, and imperative. What comes out of the overflow of our heart is what we're actually believing. But if we're actually believing, "Well, my ministry will never soar. My kids will never be saved. My body will never be healed." When that's what we're saying, then that's what our heart is going to produce. Why? Because God designed our heart to produce what we say. So, let's remain in agreement with Him and declare in every situation only what He says. Hope is like a thermostat or goal setter for what our heart can produce like good seeds in our good soil.

Would you return with me to Mark 4:26, one of our key verses? Jesus was saying, "The Kingdom of God is like a man who casts seed upon the soil. And he goes to bed at night and gets up daily and the seed sprouts and grows, how he himself does not know. This soil produces crops all by itself. First the stalk, then the head, then the mature grain in the head. When the crop permits, he immediately puts in the sickle because the harvest has come."

Not long ago, I was ministering in California when a Hispanic lady, the mother of the Associate Pastor had a damaged shoulder that was locked up. She could not raise her arm. When I touched her shoulder, she felt electricity go into her shoulder and she raised her arm with no pain. She started crying and hugging her son right in front of the audience. I discerned that faith increased substantially in the room. Did you hear faith "substance" in "substantially"?

## NOW FAITH!

For instance, when faith increased substantially, the husband whose wife had MS pushed her in the wheelchair to the front immediately. When God displays His glory, He creates faith in others and faith in Him increases substantially. Do we agree? When God reveals His glory, He creates faith in others.

Remember, I did not try to get the lady in the wheelchair to stand up, because we must work with people at the level of their faith. We studied this principle in a previous chapter. We should not tell somebody, "Throw away your medicine. Jump out of that chair. Step on your glasses." They need to develop their own personal faith on their journey. There's a big difference between acts of faith and acts of presumption.

Then in God's time, when the harvest is ready, we can stand up in the Spirit and declare, "The Lord is displaying His glory in this place." Before harvest was ready for the woman with MS, she could not stand up or raise her right arm because it was locked and atrophied. All she could do was raise her left arm. But when her harvest was ready and her faith had developed greater strength, she stood up and she raised both arms to the Lord with praise!

We need to wait on the Lord to reveal His glory! He will only reveal His glory to us individually when our personal faith is ready and revealed in our hearts. We cannot coerce anything with assumed capability in our flesh. In John 6:63, Jesus confirmed this principle, "The flesh profits nothing." We should not coerce responses, or attempt to awaken with music, or manipulate by emotionalism, or compel someone to demonstrate something outwardly.

The Holy Spirit's power flows into our spirit, waiting to be disclosed in proportion to the depth of our faith. Our faith grows according to what the Word declares and in one accord with what we thoroughly believe because we have heard the Word. I believe much of the

Church waits on the verge of revival, while few demonstrate adequate courage to live and act by faith. It's like most people are waiting for something extraordinary to happen, while everything we're waiting and hoping for has been deposited inside us already.

Reviewing: our heart automatically produces what we put in our heart, our soil. Whatever we put into our heart, it's going to produce. So, what are we planting into our heart? Are we fixing our eyes on Jesus? Are we concentrating time, diligent study, and practice in the Word of God? Are we planting faith? Or are we settling for and spinning distrust, disappointment, discouragement, despair, denial, disease, or doubt? Our heart will produce automatically what we deposit into it by thinking and declaring faith and hope. That is the way God designed us.

God is faithful to His design according to 1 Corinthians 1:9-10, "God is faithful, through whom we were called into fellowship with His Son, Jesus Christ our Lord." Jesus has called us by His blood into relationship with Him and His faithfulness. When we live, walk, and remain in the Holy Spirit, God calls us deeper into relationship with Him and His faithfulness if we stay in the Spirit. Next, verse 10, "Now I urge you brothers and sisters, by the name of our Lord Jesus Christ, that you all agree, that there will be no divisions among you, but that you be made complete in the same mind and in the same judgment."

What mind is Paul describing here? The mind of the Messiah, the mind in Christ. Paul is not describing the soulish, carnal mind that one minute is over here on the bills. The next minute it's over there on the doctor. The next minute it's buried under the shouts of news. The next minute it's in conflict with your boss. That's not the mind of Christ. The goal of Christianity is that the Body of Christ functions freely and in harmony with the same mind of Christ. That is where His glory is, where revival is, where awakening is, where breakthrough is. Amen?

# NOW FAITH!

So, God's Spirit gives our spirit revelation of God's will. And our spirit never stops searching out things that are possible in God alone. Our spirit--when redeemed and purified by grace through faith and filled with overflowing love and hope--our spirit is always automatically trying to produce what God's Spirit wants to produce. According to 1 Corinthians 6:17, our born-again spirit in unity with the Spirit of God begins to cooperate to produce what the Spirit of God wants to produce in us. But it needs the seeds of faith and hope that will unlock and release the glory.

We realize from 1 Corinthians 3:16, "We are the temple of the Holy Spirit." Therefore, the Holy Spirit, the life-giving breath, wind, and fire of God, lives in us! As Ephesians 1:3 notes, "We have every spiritual blessing in the heavenlies." This spiritual blessing (Greek = pneumatikos) produces supernatural blessing, not cursing, but overflowing blessing in the heavenly realm. Where is the heavenly realm? In the spirit realm. Where did Jesus say the heavenly realm is? In us. He is in us! (Luke 17:21). Amen?

The moment we're born again and redeemed by God, the Spirit of the Lord moves into us and we become part of His spirit realm. Then, we start to receive every spiritual, supernatural blessing. The Spirit in us begins to draw us deeper, closer to Jesus and He shows He can cleanse, purify, sanctify, and fill us with Himself. All of this is in our spirit because we began to live in the heavenlies. In Ephesians 1:13 Paul writes that once this grace is in you, it's sealed by the Holy Spirit in you. My imagination notes this is like being vacuum-sealed in one of those plastic bags when we put food in the freezer.

Our spirit within the heavenly realm where all the supernatural blessings reside now desires to produce those blessings also in the natural realm. Those blessings were sealed inside the Spirit of God, and He is now sealed inside us. 1 John 5:18-21 reassures that when we remain covered by the blood of Jesus and filled with the Spirit, the enemy can no longer possess our spirit. So, that's why the evil one continues to attempt to attack and delude our thoughts. If the accuser can persuade and delude us to think contrary to the mind of Christ, that distraction keeps the power squelched when, in fact, we could change the world inside our spirit.

1 Corinthians 2:11-13 is another one of my favorite passages defining this principle, "For who among people knows the thoughts of a person except the spirit of the person that's in him. So also the thoughts of God no one knows except the Spirit of God. Now we have not received the spirit of the world, but the Spirit who is from God, so that we may know things freely given to us by God. We also speak these things, not in words taught by human wisdom, but in words taught by the Spirit, combining spiritual thoughts with spiritual words."

What do these verses mean? The moment we're born again, and God moves inside our spirit, we become His home. Now we can know more of His thoughts because we have His Spirit, and our thoughts are controlled and enlivened by His Spirit. Eternal life is to know Him. For eternity, as we remain in Him and He fills us, we will know His thoughts more and more and more. The message of the Spirit for the Body of Messiah is not man's wisdom. We believe that since God moved into us by His Spirit, we can know His thoughts, which can produce spiritual blessing in us and speak supernatural words through us. And our words will produce the same things that His words did in Christ. That's the message of the Spirit to the Body of Christ.

We can live by the Spirit in our spirit, empowered by the Spirit, in step with the Spirit, following the Spirit, without pursuing distracting rabbit trails where we are dominated by the soul and where we swirl downward into worry and anxiety. When we abide and remain in the Spirit and know the mind of Christ, we can hear the thoughts of Christ, our words will replicate and represent the power of Christ. This is the mystery of faith and hope: Christ is in us! Hope longs and desire grows to let Him out with love, joy, peace, and patience. We declare and share His glory through the power of our words. Amen?

The spirit of wisdom is repeated in Proverbs 20:27, "The spirit of a man is the lamp of God searching all the inward parts." Our spirit is the capacity that God created to illuminate God Himself deeper into our spirit. Our spirit is the showcase for God to reveal His glory to the world. Our spirit is the lamp of God.

We can sit still and agree with God to speak His Word into our heart. We can sow a seed of faith into our spirit. Then, our spirit can start to search the Spirit of God, hoping to know how to produce good fruit that remains. This is true even when we sleep. Again, "The kingdom of God is like a person who goes around sowing seed, and then goes to bed. He himself doesn't know how it works." But his spirit knows the mind of Messiah.

Our Spirit starts searching the Spirit of God. Because once the seed is in us, the spirit goes to work as the production center to produce the seed. We know why the seed of the Spirit is called faith: even and especially when we're in pain, we desire to say with our human lips, "I'm healed. I am whole." And as pain continues, we declare with faith overflowing with hope, "Thank you, Lord, for all You are doing in my spirit, soul, and body." That is the law of faith, the principle of faith overflowing with hope.

When our checking account is overdrawn, the last thing our human lips tend to say is "I am grateful and blessed in the provisions of God." When in our congregations the numbers, noses, and nickels are decreasing, the last thing our human lips tend to say is, "Our congregation is awakening and experiencing revival." Do we agree? That's faith with hope because we're not saying what we see. We're saying what we hope for based on what we hear the Word of God saying. We live by faith overflowing with hope and not by sight.

I sense we are gaining traction together, aren't we? Now, let's return to the passage in Mark 4. We see the soil automatically produces what we put in it. Guarding our mouth from saying things contrary to the Word of God is essential and vital. Think about it. We are either planting weeds or good seeds. Do you agree we prefer to plant crops with good seeds? By grace through faith and hope, we can live in the abundance of the harvest of what God's Word is ready, willing, and able to produce in us. Amen?

Let's consider 1 Corinthians 2:14 in order to discern our battle more clearly. "A natural person does not accept the things of the Spirit of God." When we're trying to be proved by senses, everything we're embracing and practicing in the Word sounds ludicrous. That's the natural mindset. The natural, carnal person in us that lives by what our five senses can prove cannot and does not accept the things of the Spirit. Spiritual truth is foolishness to that carnal person who cannot understand them because they are spiritually discerned.

We cannot experience the supernatural unless we experience spiritual truth supernaturally. We cannot experience the supernatural power of God intellectually. We can experience spiritual truth only in our spirit. Carnality in human nature blurs and blocks our receptivity to revelation, spiritual, supernatural truth. As long as we're waiting for proof, we're going to be waiting for proof a long time. We walk by faith, not by sight.

The Word continues: "But the one who is spiritual discerns all things, yet he himself is discerned by no one." We can be in the middle of an experience that's so uncomfortable in our flesh and wonder momentarily, "What is this?" Then, the Spirit enables our spirit to discern the motivation of that experience quickly. We can learn to

# NOW FAITH!

live sincerely by the Spirit in arenas that we're not comfortable with. We can discern spirits, because our spirit is activated to produce what the Word of God says, not what our fears shout, or our religious upbringing persuades, or our culture of comfort twists.

This truth is urgent, friends. Do we realize how acutely the Church is likely to change in the next months? Unless we grow and remain together in the Word and the Spirit of the Lord, it is likely very few persons somewhat comfortable in the Body of Christ now will continue to be comfortable with the way the Church looks one year from now. Moral, cultural, and social norms are changing at light speed now. In the recent past, many among us grew accustomed to be and do what other people taught, instead of the Way in Jesus that the Spirit teaches. Jesus is getting His Bride ready. Someday soon, the Bride and the Spirit will say, "Come! Maranatha!" When Messiah returns, He will have his way with His Body. And His Bride is going to lead and reign with final authority in the Holy Spirit.

"The one who is spiritual discerns all things, yet he himself is discerned by no one. For who has known the mind of the Lord that He will instruct him, but we have the mind of Christ." Whoa! We are so blessed to believe, receive, and proclaim these Bible truths, friends! So, what we plant into our human spirit makes our spirit the "production center" and our spirit discerns all things (1 Corinthians 12:10).

As we have repeated consistently, our heart is the soil that receives the seed of faith and hope, then enables it to grow. So, we need to be careful and diligent to sow good seed and not be lazy. Hear this parenthetical Proverb in 22:13 that applies here: "A lazy person says, 'There's a lion outside.'" Doesn't that appear to be a senseless statement? A lazy person says, "The economy will never come back. The government can never turn around. Real revival can never come to our country. Our church is done; it's an old wineskin." A lazy person speaks naïve and foolish words, statements that exalt satan, instead of words that magnify the Lord. That is being spiritually lazy! Lazy people who might think they are spiritually minded and motivated, sometime speak flippant, foolish words that result in magnifying the power of satan. They fail to honor or exalt the Lord.

So, we should never say many or any words that stop our production center or our soil from automatically producing the seed of God's Word that totally intends to produce itself. We should always speak in the power of the Spirit a few words of faith, hope, and love in Jesus that will overcome. Do we agree?

Our thermostat controls the heat of the air conditioning unit. I came home one night not long ago to celebrate my wife's birthday. As soon as I walked into our home, the temperature was hot in February: 64 degrees in Kansas in the middle of winter. That's not normal. Usually, it's cold and blustery in February. So, I turned the air conditioner on and set the thermostat to 69. That little thermostat controls my big 3.5-ton unit. The unit only produces toward a goal and my thermostat is the goal setter. Hope is the goal setter that releases the power of faith so our heart can automatically produce what God's Word declares. If we don't have a thermostat, a hope, or a goal, then our power sits idle.

Every person reading this book has the same power that raised Jesus from the dead. That power is inside our spirit, waiting to be unleashed through the seeds that will release power already inside us. Each of us already has that power in Christ's death and resurrection!

Our words set the thermostat of overflowing faith to the temperature we desire. And hope is our thermostat. Our words are goal setters. We need to send a simple, clear spiritual impulse into our heart by our words. We set our goals by what we say. "Faith is the substance of things hoped for." Our voice can create hope in our heart that creates

# NOW FAITH!

faith that manifests the Word of God. Faith is the divine energy of God. Our "spirit-unit" will not produce anything without the goal set properly. The thermostat is the goal setter of our hope. Our hope has substance. And hope sets a goal, that electrifies the "spirit-unit" to produce the right temperature.

God designed our hearts to replicate and reproduce the Word of God. The soil will produce whatever we plant in it. When some of us groan, "Well, mine's not working", then we just planted unbelief and doubt with those faithless words. We can see how easy it is to become double-minded.

This statement should resonate loudly in our heads and hearts right now: we can see how easy it is to become double-minded. Any statement that we speak without the Spirit creates division in our mind. And 1 Corinthians 1:10 reminds us that the Spirit wants all of us to have the same mind, which is the mind of Christ. The soil will produce whatever we plant in it. Any of us living in the flesh has the sad capacity plant malignancy or destruction or even evil into our heart by declaring words that are not aligned with or in agreement with the Word of God.

We conclude this chapter with Galatians 3:13, "Christ redeemed us from the curse of the law, having become a curse for us. For it is written, 'Cursed is everyone who hangs on a tree'".

Everything that the devil meant for evil is involved in the curse. Christ's sacrifice has redeemed us from all selfishness, corruption, wickedness, and deceit. He's redeemed us from physical poverty, spiritual poverty, financial poverty, emotional poverty, and everything that tore us down from the pristine creation that God created humanity to become on this planet. Christ's sacrifice has redeemed us from that curse. We need to believe that. We need to believe the Word of God over our thoughts, above our emotions, over our trauma, above our pain, over our disappointment, and above our delays. We need to believe the Word of God.

Jesus declared, "It is finished. I redeem you. I restore your identity. Live by the Spirit. Grow your faith. Start saying what I say, and I will do what I do. If you say what I say and believe the truth, I'll do what I do, and you can receive it." That's the goal of faith overflowing with hope! Amen?

# 11
# BELIEVING AND CONFESSING GOD'S WORD WORK TOGETHER

Now we learn together how faith and confession cooperate, collaborate, and grow together, hand in hand. We will discover seven reasons we cannot separate faith and confession. In agreement, let's declare aloud: confessing faith works inseparably and miraculously.

Let's begin with God's Word in Matthew 13:18, "Listen, then, to the parable of the sower. When anyone hears the Word of the Kingdom and does not understand it, the evil one comes and snatches away what has been sown in his heart. This is the one sowing with seed beside the road. The one sowing with seed on rocky places is the one who hears the word and immediately receives it with joy, yet he has no firm root in himself, but it is only temporary. Then, when affliction or persecution occurs because of the word, immediately he falls away." That's interesting, isn't it?

With those verses, we link Luke 10:42, "Only one thing is necessary. Mary has chosen the good part, which shall not be taken away from her." Jesus knows that many people like to hear momentarily, receive quickly, and return to business as usual. But when we're willing to sit still, saturate, abide in, and become one with the Word, then neither the enemy nor circumstances can steal faith easily. Then, hope can take root, start producing a harvest, and nothing can stop what God intends to establish. This is biblical foundation for seven reasons faith and confession work together inseparably.

Recently, during a leadership meeting at IHOP-KC, more than 300 leaders gathered in the best-attended leadership meeting they have experienced to date. At the end of the 90-minute meeting, Mike Bickle asked me to share what I thought. After the meeting, I heard a word of knowledge and discernment from the Lord for a leader in the room. That word goes along with the passage we just read in Matthew 13.

I had been sitting in the back, visualizing what could happen while 100 million believers globally were about to pray and fast for 21 days with a passion for the salvation of Israel based on Isaiah 62. We believed revival would be unleashed, the Lord would return, and we would actually see His purposes in us and experience what the Bible says is going to happen.

So, I was sitting there when suddenly the Lord seemed to shine a spotlight on a man in the room whom I did not know. He had a beard and looked like a bodybuilder with huge arms like trees. I asked one of my friends, "What is that man's name up there who looks like a bodybuilder?" My friend replied, "Oh, that's Jacob."

So, I called his name, "Jacob!" He simply looked at me and said, "Yeah." I called, "Come here. I'm supposed to tell you something." He walked back and I spoke these words into his heart, "I don't know you. My friend told me your name is Jacob." He responded again simply, "Yeah."

Then I said, "This is what the Lord tells me about you. You have a sincere, burning passion to walk in His power to release signs, wonders, healing, and to do what Jesus did. You believe that His

# NOW FAITH!

call drives and motivates you. You can't get enough of seeing God miraculously transform people. But you're going through a 'weaker-than-ever-season' in your life right now. You feel that God's presence and power is further from you than He has ever been. You feel discouraged."

As I spoke those words into Jacob's spirit, he started crying. That big muscle-bound bodybuilder was crying tears that were falling on my hands. He kept looking at me while he was weeping. I looked into his eyes and said, "I want to give you some good news. Do you want to know the reason you're in this dry season? God is establishing your root system. You were not ready to walk in what your heart desires. You were not ready to overcome what the enemy is going to throw at you. God intends to release His power into you. Like, He wants to do this. He had to prepare your roots so the tree can stand the assault. When you get through this season, you will walk in grace, faith, and love more than you could ever ask or imagine."

We stood there a second, just looking at each other, then Jacob reached out those massive arms and hugged me. You know, he was really strong! He gave me a huge man-hug. Then, he admitted, "I needed to hear that more than you will ever know."

Well, that story illustrates these verses. Sometimes, when we're doing the hard work of confessing things when we feel nothing, then confessing more stuff when we see nothing, we're laying the root system so that the law of faith, the principles of the kingdom, can work. In seasons like those, especially when we see no outward evidence, we need to remain full of faith overflowing with hope. We need to do the hard work right then and there. Amen?

Now, let's receive by faith from the Holy Spirit into our spirit seven reasons why believing and confessing God's Word works. Are we ready to receive?

**Reason One**: Believing and confessing God's Word works, because His Word sows seeds in the Kingdom of God. Yes: faith-filled and faith-declaring seeds in the Kingdom of God. Let's receive again one of my favorite examples in Mark 4:26-29 where Jesus was saying, "The kingdom of God is like a man who cast seeds upon the soil. He goes to bed at night and gets up daily. The seed sprouts and grows, how he himself does not know. The soil produces crops all by itself. First the stalk, then the head, then the mature grain in the head. Now, when the crop permits, he immediately puts in the sickle, because the harvest has come."

What is the first thing that confessing God's Word accomplishes? Why does that work? Because that's the way we sow seeds into His Kingdom. That's the way we get seeds into the Kingdom. Now, where is His Kingdom? In the believer's heart, in the believer's spirit, which is our soil. When we speak God's Word, those seeds go into the Kingdom, which is the soil of our heart. And if we'll let those words remain, germinate, grow, and do their work, they automatically produce the substance of the seed, and fulfill the reason the seed was sown.

Hebrews 10:23 reverberates this principle: "Let's hold firmly to the confession of our hope." We remember that "faith is the substance things we're hoping for. So, "Let's hold firmly to the confession of our hope, without wavering, for He who promised is faithful." God will perform His Word when we hold unswervingly to the hope we're confessing. The first reason confessing God's Word works is that it sows seeds in the Kingdom of God.

**Reason Two**: Here is the second of seven reasons why believing and confessing God's Word works. Faith comes from hearing. Let's note Romans 10:17, "So faith comes from hearing and hearing by the word of Christ." Anytime and every time we speak God's Word, we're speaking the words of Christ. We're speaking the Word of the Spirit,

## NOW FAITH!

the Word of God. That's how faith comes. If we want faith to sprout and grow, we speak the Word of Christ. On the contrary, if we want fear to come, we speak any and every other word. It's that simple. Faith will arise as long as our hearts hear the Word in our words. However, fear will increase as long as our hearts hear everything except the Word in our words.

By now we know that "faith is the substance of what we're hoping for", based on what the Word of God says is ours. Repeat this aloud with me: "Faith is the substance of what we're hoping for", based on what God's word says is ours. Awesome!

But fear is the substance of what we say when we don't really want it to happen. So, we should not speak that. We should only declare what we desire to happen. Agree? Another verse that expands this second principle is Romans 10:8, "The word is near you, in your mouth, and in your heart. That is the word of faith, which we are preaching." That's amazing. Paul writes that the Word is near us and in our mouth so we can plant it in our heart. Do we receive this?

We repeat and remember, the word is near us, in our mouth, waiting on us to make it a part of our heart by our confessing the Word of God. We add to these two verses another one of my favorite truths in Isaiah 59:21 where the LORD God promises, "I will establish My covenant with them as an everlasting covenant." What is this everlasting covenant? God commits to plant His words in our mouth, in our children's mouth, in our grandchildren's mouth, in our great grandchildren's mouth, as an everlasting covenant.

Here is the glory of what we're living in right now, in this covenant of the Holy Spirit, being one with God, being the body of Christ, being the bride of Christ. We have God's Word in our mouth, waiting for us to plant it in our heart. That's how faith rises. How much faith do we want to operate in? How much more faith do we long to receive?

Come on! Every one of us has been given a measure of faith, but we're only operating with the measure we plant in our heart. All the issues of life come from our heart. We have a freewill and we can plant as much of God's Word in our heart as we choose to.

**Reason Three**: Why does believing and confessing God's Word work? It renews our mind to think like God the Father and Jesus His Son. Let's gaze into Proverbs 23:7 first, "As a man thinks within himself, so he is." What we believe and confess, what we think produces what we say. Right? Now let's add Romans 12:2, "Do not be conformed to this world." What does that mean? Don't be pressed into the mold of this world. Don't be characterized by the nature or image or likeness of a dark-world-system of deciding, thinking, behaving, or feeling.

Paul continues, "but be transformed by the renewing of your mind." How are we transformed? By allowing God's Word to empower us to live like God and Jesus by entire renewal of our spirit through the Spirit's cleansing, purifying, and filling. He plants and pours His Spirit into our spirit and enables us to receive the mind of Christ. Then, we no longer decide, think, or feel like our old natural, carnal self. This is so important. What we're probing and proving here is simple and significant.

Many Christians are double-minded: they have the mind of Christ in their spirit because God lives in them. But much of the time, they allow the natural, selfish, flesh-controlled, carnal mind to make the decisions of their life, even though their spirit attempts to persuade them how better to live. They don't invest time to plant the Word of God in their heart. If they would invest time with the Lord and in the Word, they could learn to agree with the single-mindedness of Christ and stop being double-minded.

What does believing and confessing God's Word accomplish? It helps us to start thinking like Jesus. How we think is extremely important:

our thought life is one of the most powerful forces on earth. Our thought life will either help us believe what God's Word says is our reality, or what every other word says is our reality. What we believe, confess, and think determines most of our decisions: what we become, what we say, what we do, where we go, and why.

Let's return to and finish Romans 12:2, "Do not be conformed to this world, but be transformed by the renewing of your mind, so you may prove what is the will of God, that which is good, acceptable, and perfect." We don't have to wonder, and we don't have to guess, because the renewing of our mind will help us "prove what is the will of God, that which is good." The more we put God's Word in our mind, the closer we can get to the bullseye of why God created us to be on this planet. That is our identity, our true spiritual value. Let that truth sink in by reading it again! The more we put God's Word in our mind, the closer we can get to the bullseye of why God created us to be on this planet, because we can operate in God's good will. Then, we can get closer to the heart by understanding and His acceptable will. If we keep transforming our lives by the renewing of our mind through the power of God's Word, we all can find God's perfect will for our lives. That is good news!

Before we go on, let's remember that believing and confessing God's Word by renewing our mind is to think like God the Father and Jesus His Son. Add John 1:1, "In the beginning was the Word." Now that's the Logos, the thoughts of God. In the beginning, God was thinking. "In the beginning was the Word, and the Word was with God. And the Word was God." That Word was and is spoken. So, in the beginning, God had thoughts that produced words. What God was thinking motivated Him to start speaking.

Then, "All things came into being through Him." When God started speaking, that spoken word produced the Word, which became flesh. "And the Word became flesh, and dwelt among us, and we saw

His glory as of the Son from the Father full of grace and truth" (John 1:14). That same pattern parallels the development of our faith. We start with our thoughts, which produce our words, which manifest in the natural, in our flesh. For all of us, that is the journey of faith, and it starts with our thought life.

What is the necessity of believing and confessing God's Word? We start to think like Jesus. When we think like Jesus, we'll learn to talk like Jesus. Then, as we talk like Jesus, we'll demonstrate results like Jesus. God created us in His image and gave us new birth through His Son in order to do this!

**Reason Four**: Believing and confessing the Word of God keeps the answer available in front of us. Do we know where our faith stops? Faith stops at our questioning. That's where faith halts. "I wonder if my family will ever be saved. I wonder if my family will ever be healed. I wonder if our relationship will ever be restored. I wonder if my ministry will ever blossom. I wonder if my business will ever take off. I wonder if I will ever receive healing." Our questioning is where our faith stops. Come on!

Believing and confessing God's Word always keeps the answer obtainable, in front of us. Are you blessed by this like I am? Mark 1:40, "A man with leprosy came to Jesus imploring Him, and kneeling down and saying to Him, 'If you're willing, you can make me clean.'" This man believes God can cleanse him. But the man questions whether he wants to be clean. He believes God can. But he wonders whether he wants God to do what he knows God can do.

This kind of questioning might describe much of the Church. Most of us believe God can do anything. We know He can. We know He can do anything. Most of us question whether He really wants to Do we know why we question? Because we have not spent enough time in the Word, which would answer that question. When we invest time

# NOW FAITH!

with the Lord and in the Word, we would never wonder whether God sincerely wants to do what His Word promises to do.

In order to comprehend the irony of this, watch how Jesus responds to this man in Mark 1:41, "Moved with compassion…" Aren't you glad Jesus is drawn to our belief that He wants, that He can, or even our doubt that He will? And when we come to Him, He is always moved with compassion. "And He touched him and said to him, 'I am willing, be cleansed.' Immediately, the leprosy left him, and he went away cleansed."

When was the man healed? When Jesus touched him? No. He was healed when Jesus answered his question by declaring, "I am willing." As soon as Jesus answered his question, immediately the man's faith seized the Word, believed the Word, and he was cleansed. Then, he started confessing! Jesus is the answer. Do you remember this old song? "Jesus is the answer for the world today. Above Him there's no other. Jesus is the way!" He is the only answer to all questions that stop our faith.

Now, let's add 2 Corinthians 4:16-18, "Therefore, we do not lose heart. Though our outer person is decaying, yet our inner person is being renewed day by day. For our momentary, light affliction is producing for us an eternal weight of glory, far beyond all comparison. While we look not at the things that are seen, but the things that are not seen. For the things that are seen are temporal. For the things that are not seeing are eternal."

What does believing and confessing God's Word do? This consistent commitment helps us focus on things we cannot see yet. Believing and confessing gives us this assurance: that is what we will eventually see when we keep believing! The more we confess God's Word, the more He keeps the answer accessible and achievable.

In Mark 11:23-24, we read Jesus said, "Truly I say to you, whoever says to this mountain be taken up and thrown into the sea, and does not doubt in his heart, but believes that what he says is going to happen." That means it hasn't happened. That means we can't see it yet. We're not focusing on the mountain, even though we know it's not moving. We're focusing on the power that God speaks, the same power our words have when you believe in our heart, and we don't doubt or question. We focus on what you cannot yet see!

Believing and confessing God's Word keeps the answer before us and blurs the problem blocking the way. When we believe and confess God's word, we magnify the Lord and His answer. When we profess our problems, we aggrandize the devil and complicate the problem. We must choose to believe and confess that whatever God says is going to happen: "It will be granted to him. Therefore, I say to you, all things for which you pray and ask, believe that you have received them, and they will be granted to you."

**Reason Five**: Believing and confessing God's Word works! In what way? It changes our heart. I've talked with a lot of people about this who say, "Well, I tried that, but it didn't work." Do you know why? Because they are looking for the outward manifestation first. Now faith--faith in every now--works immediately, although it might not be visible instantly. What do believing and confessing accomplish? Changing us! Us! Now! Before we see a miracle, before we see a breakthrough, before we see prosperity, faith in God's Word starts changing us! We are the issue! God's Word helps us! Aren't we glad?

Proverbs 4:20 teaches, "My son (or daughter), pay attention to My words. Incline your ear to My sayings. They are not to escape from your sight. Keep them in your heart, for they are life to those who find them and healing to all their body." Isn't that a good promise? When we keep the Word before us, when we keep the Word in our vision, when keep the Word in our hearing, when we keep confessing the Word, and we keep on keeping the Word before us, it finds us and we will find it. And it will give us eternal life, which is spiritual life. And it will give us health in all our body. Like, it changes us. God's Word changes us! Come on!

Why is this important? Let's keep reading Proverbs 4:23, "Watch over your heart, with all diligence, for from it flow all the issues of your life." So, when we keep confessing God's Word, eventually our heart will be transformed. God's Word promises this. Every area of our life will benefit. This starts by changing our heart. Amen?

The singer writes in Psalm 45:1, "My heart is moved with a good theme. I address my verses to the king. My tongue is the pen of a ready writer." When we have a good theme, it's the Word of God, the declarations we're eager to repeat aloud to our King. When that happens, our mouth starts imprinting God's Word on our heart. Simultaneously! God's Word has the purpose and power to change our hearts!

Proverbs 3:1-3 instructs, "My son (or daughter), do not forget My teachings. But have your heart comply with My commandments, for length of days and years of life and peace they will add to you." What will add to us? God's Word, His commandments will add length of days and peace to us. The outcome will be much more than mere survival; it will be abundant living. Verse 3: "Do not let kindness and truth leave you. Bind them around your neck. Write them on the tablet of your heart." How can we do that? By believing and confessing God's Word.

What is the goal of confessing God's Word? Eventually, the goal is Matthew 12:34, so our mouth will start speaking out of the overflow of our heart. What will your heart be overflowing with? What we have put in it, right? The more we confess the Word, the more we declare the Word, the more we speak the Word, the more our heart is full. Gradually, our mouth will speak what is overfilling our heart. What if we become so full of the Word of God that faith in Him is all we speak? Like, that's all we can say. Here are a couple of examples.

In 2 Kings 4:23 we find the story of prophet Elisha proclaiming to a childless couple that they would birth a son. The child was born and grew, but their boy developed a severe headache and died in his mother's lap. Immediately, the mother asked her husband to send for Elisha. But her husband asked, "Why are you going to him today. This is neither a new moon nor Sabbath. She replied, "That's alright."

This mother is so confident in the power of God that she responds simply that it's alright. Her son is dead, but "It will be fine." She is either crazy, delusional, or her heart is filled with faith. I'm going with her heart is filled with faith. Come on! She saddled her donkey and set out without slowing down to see Elisha herself. Now, skip ahead to 4:26. Elisha saw her and said to his servant, "Please run now to meet her and ask her, "Are you alright? Is your husband alright? Is your son alright?" She answered, "Everything is alright." Twice in this story when her son was dead, the Mama was saying, "Everything is alright."

Confessing God's Word has capacity, power, and authority to change our heart. So even in the worst of circumstances, we believe and confess God's Word. I'm fired up right now. What if we become so stuffed with truth of the Word, so expectant in God's Word that even when, not if, all hell breaks out against us, then we respond with the Word of God! All we have to respond with is the Word of God. Not our opinion about it, not our track record, but His track record!

What if when our child is dead, our business is lost, our ministry is failing, our health is setback, and our finances are a wreck, we still say, "Everything is alright." How? Why? Because God said He would never leave us or forsake us. He's with us to the end. What if that became our reality? It could be if we never stopped confessing God's Word. Amen? Amen!

**Reason Six**: Why does believing and confessing God's Word work? It sets the law of faith in motion. It's a law or principle. We note Romans 3:27, "Where then is boasting? It has been excluded. By what kind of law? Of works? No. But by a law of faith." And verse 31, "Do we then nullify the law through faith? Far from it! On the contrary, we establish the law."

What is the law we establish? The law of faith. How do we establish faith? By speaking words that cause faith to rise. "Faith comes by hearing." The heart is changed by hearing and believing. Our thinking is changed by hearing and believing. We wait on the Lord to write His Word on our heart, so that His Word fills our heart. This is based on our willingness to confess the Word instead of confessing fear. Confessing and professing the Word of God establishes the law of faith in us. Amen?

Let's go back to Mark 11 again, because every one of us faces a mountain right now in our life. Instead of being intimidated by the mountain, we should speak to it. Jesus teaches us with truth in Mark 11:23, "Whoever says to this mountain, 'Be taken up and thrown into the sea…'" The Lord does not say: whoever thinks that the mountain should move. He doesn't say: whoever helps the mountain to move. Jesus declares, "Whoever says to this mountain, 'Be taken up and cast into the sea', and does not doubt in his heart, but believes that what he says is going to happen, it will be granted to him."

How and when are we ever going to stop doubting in our heart? When our heart is filled completely with the Word of God because we planted it in our heart by confessing and professing the Word by faith. God's Word is true! How and when are we ever going to get to the place where we can speak to impossible situations with no doubt? When we fill our heart with nothing but the truth of God's Word. Come on!

Paul wrote in Romans 12:3, "God has given all of us a measure of faith." Is each of us glad that we have received some measure of faith? But do we know that the measure we're working with is determined by how much of the faith of God's Word we put in our heart? Again, every one of us has been given a measure of faith. And the level of faith we're operating at is dependent on how much of God's Word we put in our heart. The Word of God does not get into us by itself. We have to plant it in there day by day. Amen!

Do you remember when the apostles asked Jesus for more faith? In Luke 17:5-6, He says that we don't need huge faith. We need "faith as a mustard seed. Then, we can say to this mulberry tree, 'Be uprooted and planted in the sea' and it will obey you." What was he saying about a mustard seed? A mustard seed faith is one of the few plants on the planet that cannot be cross-pollinated. Scientists can cross and produce hybrid corn, beans, beets, onions, leeks, bananas, peppers, and so on. But we cannot cross-pollinate mustard seed. It won't cross-pollinate.

What was Jesus saying? When we need faith that uproots trees, when we need faith to move mountains, and when we need faith to accomplish impossible solutions, only one seed source will produce what we need. That's the Word of God. We cannot have faith based on what God's Word says plus what somebody else says. God's Word cannot be cross- pollinated. Pure, authentic faith comes from the pure, authorized Word of God.

In Leviticus 19:19, the LORD God says that we're never supposed to plant mingled seed: cross-pollinated or hybrid seed. Why? Because that seed will produce a harvest only one time. And then it goes back to its original seed. It cannot keep producing the same harvest.

# NOW FAITH!

God does not want a "one-and-done" harvest lifestyle. God wants us to live in a harvest that keeps producing, keeps producing, keeps producing, so that the goodness and mercy of God overtakes us. And it's no longer us, but it's Christ in us that's compelling us to do these things. But that will never happen if we're planting seeds and weeds at the same time. There's only one source of pure seed: it's imperishable and incorruptible. It's the Word of God.

We learn faith in Romans 10:17, "Faith comes by hearing, and hearing by the word of Christ." We learn faith in Mark 9:23, "Nothing is impossible for those who believe." We learn faith in Matthew 4:4, "Man does not live on bread alone, but on every word that proceeds from the mouth of the Father." We learn faith in John 6:63 where Jesus says, "The flesh profits nothing. My words are spirit and life. We learn faith in Romans 10:8, "The word is near you: it's in your mouth, so you can put it in your heart. This is the word of faith that we're preaching to you."

Again, the sixth reason believing and confessing God's Word works: it sets the law of faith in motion. Wouldn't it be better if we believed and aligned and spoke this principle and law, enabling God to work instead of us thinking most of the time we have to work? You see, when we fulfill the law of faith, we depend on God completely, we draw from His resources consistently. And this principle fulfills the truth that "His yoke is easy, and His burden is light."

By God's grace, we can move into faith and out of striving, into faith and out of performing, into faith and out of false flattery and seduction that many people in the Church live in. We can fulfill the law of faith. We can put the Word of God to the test, not rebelliously, but faithfully! By God's grace, we can "seek first the kingdom of God and His righteousness." It is God's pleasure to take care of all the ways the devil wants us to worry. God wants to take care of that. This is good news. Amen!

**Reason Seven:** Why does believing and confessing God's Word work? As we study His Word, God releases angels to help us. Hebrews 1:14 asks, "Are not all angels ministering spirits set out to provide service for the sake of those who will inherit salvation?" Yes! Every angel has an assignment to help us who believe, receive, and profess salvation.

Most of us remember the first few verses of Psalm 103, right? "Bless the Lord, oh my soul, and all that is within me, bless His holy name. Bless the Lord, all my soul, and forget not all His benefits, who heals all our diseases and forgives all our sins." We love the first few verses, but we might forget Psalms 103:20, "Bless the Lord, you His angels, mighty in strength, who perform his Word, obeying the voice of His Word."

Do we sincerely believe the Holy Bible is the Word of God? Would you put your Bible up to your ear now and listen for it to make a sound. No, there's no sound. It's not like a seashell. It does not have a voice. But when we speak the Bible aloud with our heart and lips, we give voice to the Word of God. Then, He sends His angels to perform the Word of God on our behalf. Millions of angels are eager to hear the heart of the Lord, waiting for someone to declare the Word of God. He is for us, not against us. So, angels are for us, not against us. When we know and love God and speak His word with faith, we are in the majority, and He releases angels to confirm His majority presence and power.

In Luke 12:8 Jesus proclaimed, "Now I say to you, everyone who confesses me before people, the Son of Man will also confess Him before the angels of God." Read and think about that verse. What does that verse mean for each of us? When we're with people, we will have an opportunity often to speak what God's Word declares more than what our circumstances shout. Perhaps our economy is ruined,

## NOW FAITH!

or our business is a wreck, or our ministry is in trouble, or our kids are disobedient and distant, or our health is weak.

Then, instead of speaking words of fear or doubt like what most people typically say, let's decide now to start confessing God's Word to them and with them. For example, we might ask, "Would you like to know what a verse in the Bible teaches about this problem?" When we are with other people, the moment we give God's Word voice, we release His authority, and we access audience with angels who are mighty in strength and eager to perform and fulfill His Word. Hallelujah!

As we wrap up this chapter, let's review why believing and confessing God's Word works.

- Reason one: His Word sow seeds in the Kingdom of God.
- Reason two: faith comes from hearing.
- Reason three: His Word renews our mind to start thinking like God.
- Reason four: it keeps the answer available, obtainable, in front of us at all times.
- Reason five: it changes our heart.
- Reason six: it sets the law of faith in motion.
- Reason seven: it releases angels to help us.

Speaking words of faith will not automatically make something happen. But declaring the Word of God with faith is a huge step toward enabling something extraordinary to happen. When we need a miracle any day, let's decide now to do whatever Jesus says. Let's do whatever He says. Jesus released miracles by what He said. We and others receive miracles by doing what He said.

Remember John 2:5. Jesus and his disciples are at a wedding. All the guests had consumed all the wedding wine. His mother Mary said, "Jesus, they're out of wine." Jesus responded, "It is not my time yet. Why do you care, mother?" Mary simply turned to the disciples and spoke with faith, "Do whatever He says." She spoke faith in the Word, because she knew the miracle was possible if they would do whatever Jesus said.

Bottom line: the Lord Jesus will perform more miracles through our lives when we do whatever He says.

# 12

# DECLARING BY FAITH THE WORD OF GOD OVER OURSELVES

We started this journey together to discover how to live by faith, how to fulfill the law of faith, how to agree with God's Word and actions in Jesus, and how to unlock what He put in motion from the beginning of creation. Part of the catalyst for this series of messages is in Luke 18:8 when Jesus asked, "When the Son of Man returns, will even find faith on the earth?" That has been a burning motivation in my heart.

With that question, Jesus expressed concern about the impatient desires of so many people for instant solutions, delays from distractions, too many conflicting options, speed of information and knowledge, increase of wickedness, and love of most people growing cold. If Jesus is concerned, we should be ready, willing, and able to "fight the good fight of faith" and to be sure we are living by faith in Him and His Word when he returns. That has been one of many motivations for these lessons, not the only purpose, but one of many concerns that drew us together through these chapters.

Several times, I have mentioned the evening our daughter-in-law invited us for spaghetti dinner. She asked our granddaughter to take a string of spaghetti out of the pot and said, "Throw it on the wall. If it sticks, it's ready." Similarly, I intended to describe faith from many different angles, hoping one of them will stick. The Lord also hopes each of us receives and believes these truths and starts to live by faith instead of by feelings. The fight of faith is overcoming feelings that take us out of the spirit as well as maximizing feelings that help us go deeper into the spirit. That's the fight of faith. We don't want to ignore or negate feelings, but neither do we want to let negative feelings talk us out of who the Word of God says we are.

Let's start this chapter by declaring, speaking confidently: God wants each of us to hear His Word. Let's speak that audibly now: God wants each of us to hear His Word. "Faith comes by hearing and hearing by the Word of God" (Romans 10:17). So, the more we hear His Word, the more we receive faith. The more we receive faith, the more faith grows. Some of us can record or play a recording of Scripture, repeating it over and over again.

Yet, the best way to develop a lifestyle of believing and confessing God's Word is by implementing and obeying it to the best of our ability. This requires daily discipline. Nobody else will do this for us. The Holy Spirit will help us develop discipline to implement a Joshua 1:8 lifestyle, "Do not let this book of the law depart from your mouth. Be careful to meditate on it day and night. Be careful to do all that is written in it, so your way will be prosperous and everything you do will be successful." The part of that verse I want to emphasize in this teaching on faith is to practice meditating on the Word of God day and night as well as to implement it with faith daily and consistently.

The word "meditate" in that verse could mean to muse, to ponder deeply, to chew on, or to mull over. My favorite definition of that word meditate is "to murmur or talk to yourself." Maybe an example of that in the New Testament narrative would be the lady with the issue of blood. As noted in Mark 5:28, she was saying to herself, "If I just touch the hem of His garment, I will be made whole. She did touch His prayer shawl and she was healed. She was believing a Hebrew Scripture in Malachi 4:2, which states that when the son of righteousness arises, there will be healing in His "wings", the tassels of His prayer shawl, representing His Word. She was also pursuing the instruction of Joshua 1:8, "Be careful to meditate on it day and night."

This woman spent all the money she had. She grew worse, but she recalled a verse in her Hebrew Bible. She found God's Word for her situation. She started thinking, believing, and saying words of faith. That is practicing Joshua 1:8.

Let's consider a fun example of how a cow chews the cud. I used this illustration previously, but right here it will be a good reminder. When a cow eats, it gets some grass and starts chewing. And it chews and chews. I don't know how a cow chews so much. Finally, the grass breaks down and goes into the first stomach. God designed a cow with four stomach chambers. He also created a cow to keep chewing the cud until the process leaves the first stomach to the second stomach. The second stomach will extract more nutrients.

The cow keeps chewing until saliva goes down into the digestive tract and the cud moves from the second into the third stomach. The cow keeps chewing and the cud finally gets into the fourth stomach. When it extracts everything out of the grass, that bite is finished, and the next bite begins. It's amazing that God designed a cow to be able to derive so much energy and so many nutrients out of something with zero calories that it can grow up to 1200 pounds on grass. God created a cow to extract everything out of grass. It merely keeps chewing.

Here's another funny story. Dr. Craig Rench introduced me to Clag and Kathy Offutt, some of his friends in Medford, Oregon. Kathy was a health lady, a real health specialist. I think she juiced and smoothied almost everything. The first time I walked into their home, it smelled like a vegetable greenhouse. There seemed to be little particles of celery and carrots in the air from all the juicing. I remember Kathy said, "Dan, if you want to get all possible nutrients out of a salad or similar food, you need to chew it 25 times." Then she added, hoping that Dan was curious and ready for more, "If you chew it 25 times, it releases the nitrogen out of the greens. That opens up all your arteries and you will never have a heart problem."

Well, I thought a moment and said, "Okay, I'll try it." But I could only complete about four chews. I don't know how to chew lettuce 25 times. Like, how can a person do that? I mean, just imagine: we put something in our mouth and we count 1-2-3-4 chews. Then, we swallow it. But they were telling me to chew it 25 times. Well…?

Okay, those are illustrations of Joshua 1:8. God created each of us to be able to discipline ourselves to extract every life-giving, health-giving, deliverance-giving, prosperity-giving, and every bit of spiritual, supernatural, divine DNA that's in every particle of God's Word.

Let's recall the story in Matthew 15 about the lady who knew the power of God's Word and said, "If You will give me a crumb of your Word, all my problems will be satisfied, and my demon-possessed daughter will be healed. I simply want and need a crumb of Your Word."

Jesus was serious when He was being tempted. The statement He knew from Deuteronomy 8:11, He summarized again in Matthew 4:4, "Man does not live on bread alone but on every word that comes from the mouth of God." Jesus taught that if we'll live in the promises of God, the written word, they will lead us to the Living Word. Then, we can become partakers of the divine nature and taste and see how good God really is. We already know we become what we eat. We can learn to live on every Word from God, chew on it, meditate on it, and talk to ourselves and others about it. No other person can do that for us. We must love, receive, believe, and live the Word ourselves.

# NOW FAITH!

That is why Jesus was concerned to ask, "When I return, will I find faith?" He knew how easy it would be for us to rely on second-hand words. Let that sink in. Jesus knew how easy it would be for all of us to rely on second-hand words, instead of investing time alone in the Bible, prayer, and with the Living Word. We know this challenge in our age, especially because of the increase of knowledge and the decrease of love for Him. So much information races toward us: social media, YouTube, podcasts, TV shows, radio programs, congregations, political parties, organizations, and so much more. We have so many opportunities to indulge in everything around us. We need intentionality in the secret and quiet place in our spirit so the Word in us can speak more deeply within us and enable us to overcome what's around us.

When the Lord sanctified me, baptized/immersed me in the Holy Spirit, and totally consumed me, two transformations impacted my spirit and soul more than other blessings I received and believed. First, I started understanding that the Holy Spirit of God wants to do supernatural miracles in people. I started to believe He really wants to work His power in and through me in these ways. Second, I couldn't get enough of His Word. Those two truths changed my life.

After the Lord encountered and transformed me, my dad and I remember we built a glory barn on my farm in Kansas. We began to meet with many men, all of whom longed to learn how to love Jesus more, how to hear the Holy Spirit, how to study the Word, how to pray, and how to do what Jesus does. All of us wanted more of what Jesus kept doing in and through us as we met in that barn on our farm. I would enter His presence there and enjoy half a day in the Word. I did not want to depart from His manifestations or stop hearing His voice. During those days and hours, I experienced deepening desire to know the Word in person and in print. I also read a couple thousand excellent books by extraordinary Christian authors.

I experienced authentic hunger to know Jesus; I wanted the Word to become flesh in me. Why? Because when the Word becomes flesh, then when we speak it, it becomes spirit. And the spirit is where the kingdom is, and where the kingdom is, the supernatural becomes natural. That's the goal of faith. Amen? So, Joshua says, "Be careful to meditate, murmur, repeat to yourself day and night." What we say, sets a goal. Again, when we say something, that's a goal we're setting. And hope is the ultimate goal.

Remember: we are learning about faith in this series. We return to one of the foundational verses about faith in Hebrews 11:1, "Faith is the substance of things we hope for." When we're confessing what we hope for based on God's Word, that's our goal. The goal of hope gives our spirit something to strive for, because God designed our hearts--our spiritual soil--to produce whatever seed we put in it. So, we need to express our goal by declaring our hope based on what God says is ours, not what the world says. This declaration by faith sets in motion the way God created us to extract everything out of His Word, similar to the way He created the cow to extract everything out of grass. So, we need to start saying what God says about us.

Are you sick of me repeating this principle so many times? Well, we really need to start saying what God's Word says about us, and to stop saying what Satan says about us. We need to speak truth instead of lies. The devil lies, "You're broke. You'll never get ahead. You'll never get out of the hole. You'll never be healed from this sickness. You'll never get rid of this depression. Your family will never be saved. Your ministry will never take off."

That's not at all what God says. He says the exact opposite. If we want our faith to take root in the Word of God that produces what it says, we need to start saying it, declaring it with faith. We need to say it. Does it seem that so many people are sitting around waiting for somebody to say it for them? God didn't design us to do that. God designed us to speak His Word. He puts His Word in our mouth, so we could put it in our heart. Amen? That's Romans 10:8.

Again, we need to start saying what God says about us and to stop saying what the devil says about us. We need to put a guard over our tongue because "faith comes by hearing, and hearing by the word of Christ." Fear comes by hearing, and hearing by opposing, opposite words about what we don't want to happen. But why would we think thoughts or speak words aloud that we don't want to happen? Do we really want to know? This is what I want to declare with clarity in the rest of this chapter. This is going to be so practical. I will offer an example of a confession that we can speak over our own lives every single day. Then we will study Scripture that shows us why we should be speaking what that Word declares.

Here is the goal of confessing the Word. Eventually, our heart becomes filled with the Word, and we no longer need to confess it only to put it in. We also need to confess the Word by speaking it out. Do you remember when we were young, and we needed to learn multiplication tables one through twelve? We made little flash cards and needed to repeat those tables over and over again. Right? Four times four equals 16. Five times five equals 25. Six times six equals 36. Seven times seven equals 49. Eight times eight equals 64. Got it? All of us learned multiplication tables by saying them, by speaking them, and by repeating them over and over.

Well, if we can learn multiplication tables, then we have ability to learn the Word of God by confessing it and repeating it again and again. According to Romans 12:3, God gave each of us a measure of faith when we repented, He forgave us, and we were born again. But the measure of faith we operate in is according to how much of the Word of God we've spoken into our own hearts. The measure we operate in is based on how much we plant in our own hearts by what we say.

Let's note and ponder several verses on this theme:

- Romans 10:8, "The word of God is near you, it's in your mouth and in your heart."
- Psalm 45:1, "Your tongue is the pen of a skillful writer."
- Proverbs 3:1-3, "Write God's Word on your heart."
- Proverbs 4:20-22, "Don't ever let the Word leave your eyes. Don't ever let it leave your heart. Be careful to do everything because those who find it find life and health to all their body."

We could list 100 verses like these. The goal of faith is to follow the Word by what we put into our heart so that we live a lifestyle of Matthew 12:34, "The mouth speaks out of the overflow of the heart." That's the goal of faith. When any pressure comes against us, we automatically know the antidote, the remedy, because we know the Answer. Remember: in previous chapters and teachings, we learned our faith always stops when we start questioning. But Jesus is always the Answer. His Word is always the answer to our questions.

So, if we have invested a lifetime of believing and confessing the Word, and confessing the Word, and confessing the Word, then our heart knows the answer to every circumstance that is a contradiction to the Word. And we can speak out of the overflow of our heart. What does that mean? What is filling our heart is what will come out of our heart. If fear fills our heart, fear will come out of our heart. If worries or doubts fill our heart, more worries and more doubt will come out of our heart. If the Word is filling our heart, then love, faith, and confidence will come out of our heart. Amen?

I know very few people who practice this principle, this law of faith. How do I observe this? Everywhere I go, people in congregations need revival. If they were overflowing with the Word, they would already be living revived. And they would be reviving by God's grace through faith and the power of the Holy Spirit within them: their

## NOW FAITH!

marriages, families, friends, co-workers, schools, community, and needy world systems.

This sounds so easy, but it takes discipline and diligence to practice living in the Word and the Spirit and to learn to talk to our soul through our spirit. We are glad one of the characteristics that fruit of the Spirit produces in us is self-control. We can pour as much of the Word into our hearts as we want to.

Now, I will provide an example of what it would look like to confess God's Word over ourselves day and night, day and night, day and night, never letting it depart from our eyes, from our heart, or from our mouth. I will verbalize and summarize these declarations from the Word initially. Then, we will return to the Scripture references for each of these to tie them together.

First, God will supply all my needs, according to His glorious riches in Christ Jesus. I can do all things through Christ, who strengthens me. I overcome evil with good, because I am part of the body of Christ. Greater is He who is in me than he who is in the world. So, I will fear no evil, for your Word and Spirit comfort me. I am free, so worry and fear cannot come near me. I will live and not die; I will declare the marvelous works of the Lord. Whatever I do will prosper. I am delivered from the evil of this world, so no harm can befall me or come near my tent, my household, my family. God sends His Word, and He saves me heals me, and delivers me.

As I continue in His Word, I will never experience death in spirit, because I am the head and not the tail, so I will never die spiritually. I am so blessed because I bless and give to others. I don't merely listen to the Word and become good seed in good soil, but I also take the shield of faith as a lifestyle. No arrows of the enemies can come near me because God's force field surrounds me. I am redeemed from the curse of the law. I'm healed. I'm free. I prosper. I'm alive. My words have power. I speak to mountains, and they tremble. I speak to fruitless trees, and they die. I speak to impossibilities, and they become miracle stories.

Every cell In my body obeys the Word of God. I resist the devil, and he runs from me in fear. I am not in poverty; I am blessed. I am not in sickness; I am healed. I'm not dying; I'm thriving and not merely surviving. I'm more than a conqueror. I have wealth now in life because I know God's Word and have hidden it in my heart so that I won't sin against Him. I can draw closer to Him every moment of eternity, because to know Him is eternal life. I know God's voice. I don't listen to a stranger's voice because I'm one of His sheep and His sheep know His voice. I am a sheep who knows His voice.

Believe it or not, I know all things because the Holy Spirit and His anointing lives inside me and because I'm the temple of the Holy Spirit. I am a house built for the King. I am growing up into the full measure of Christ Jesus. I am not going backwards two steps, and forward one step. I'm going from glory to glory, from truth to truth, from revelation to revelation. I can lay hands on the sick and they recover. No deadly poison could ever touch me. I can speak in a new language to persuade people I am a part of a different movement. This is not a movie; it's reality and it's been growing 2000 years.

I have authority in Christ over demons to release angels, over the power of death, over the power of sickness, and over anything that contradicts the Word of God. I will use authority in Christ to cover my family, to cover my ministry, to cover my friends, and to cover our congregation. I apply the blood of Jesus as a lifestyle. When I walk in the room, satan trembles because he knows I believe in the Word, I declare the Word with valor, and I will live forever.

Now, that is an example of what the Spirit will empower each of us to do. If we spend a lifestyle confessing God's Word, planting it

# NOW FAITH!

in our heart, then that is far better than "Hey, can you keep me in your prayers? I'm going through a rough time. Can you pray for me, because it seems I don't have an answer." We must invite the Holy Spirit, then cooperate with Him to fill our hearts until we overflow with the Word of God. So, even when "all hell is breaking loose," and we believe "all hell is going to break loose even worse", then we will not be moved from fixing our eyes on Jesus, the author and perfector of our faith.

The devil has not changed his mode of operation. He is roaming around seeking to devour every one of us. He's never going to stop. He is that persistent, but we can also be persistent in faith, we can persevere not by might or power, but by the Spirit of the LORD. We can overcome by the blood of the Lamb, by the word of our testimony, and by not loving our lives so much as to shrink from death. Nobody is going to do this for us! The Spirit gives us power and authority to do this in Him.

Now, let's note references in the Word for some of those declarations. We started off with Philippians 4:19. Aren't we glad that He supplies all our needs? We are also glad He does not supply our needs based on our needs. He supplies our needs based on His glorious riches in Christ Jesus. That means our needs aren't the biggest issue. Our trust always flows after He meets our needs. Our honesty always thrives after He meets our needs.

Then, we declared Philippians 4:13, "I can do all things through Christ who strengthens me." That is the flip side of John 15:5, "Apart from Me, you can do nothing." Many of us have that attitude: we think we're apart from Him, so we do nothing. But I like far better, "I can do all things through Christ who strengthens me," because I am in Christ and Christ is in me.

The next verse was "I overcome evil with good" (Romans 12). We don't overcome evil by anger, fighting, or revenge. For I am the body of Christ, as Paul wrote at the end of Ephesians chapter 1 and into the first half of Ephesians chapter 2. Paul says we are His body, the body of Christ. He's the head. We're the body. Now, the head can do nothing without the body and the body can do nothing without the head. That's why it's imperative that we live in Christ and Christ lives in us. So, the two become one and what He desires as the Head, the body lives out in obedience and submission to the Father.

Then, we spoke, "Greater is He who is in us" (1 John 4:4). Let's delve into that verse a little deeper and apply it to our lives. The verse starts with "Little children." We need to remain like little children, because faith doesn't come by, "Oh, yeah, I've already done that. Yeah, I've already heard that." That's not how faith comes. Faith comes when we're like a little child: when the Father speaks, we know that's life. We know that's truth. We know that's our protection. We know that's our identity. We know that's our provision. When the Father speaks, when the Word of God speaks, then our faith arises. But we will never receive faith unless we become and believe like a little child.

When we are like a little child, the reality is, "Greater is He who is in you." Now, what does that mean? He's greater than sickness. He's greater than poverty. He's greater than scandal. He's greater than sin. He's greater than disease. He's greater than depression. Come on! He's greater than lack. He's greater than demons. Either He is greater than absolutely everything, or He is not greater. The One in us is greater than everything we ever worry about, because we believe He's greater. Amen?

See, every one of these verses deserves a whole sermon by itself. I summarized a many to provide an example of what our practice in life can be like. Now, which demon do we think would want to be assigned to us if we were sending that many arrows against him every time he comes into our room at night? Let's think about that in light of who the Word is. Every imp and every fiend from hell would say, "No, I don't want to go in their room. Every time I go in there, they met me with the bright light of God's Word, and I leave all beaten up!"

I want to be a person who inflicts pain on the enemy. I do not want to be wondering, "Oh, can you keep me in your prayers?" I want to be like a child, but I don't want to act or practice small, inadequate faith. The body of Christ is greater So, I will fear no evil. Your Word and your Spirit comfort me. There are so many. We could pour out all of Psalm 118 about the Word. And we find nine different words to describe the Word in Psalm 119, repeating over and over again: truth, precepts, statutes, they're all about God's word. This is comfort. It is light. It is hope.

Then, I'm free. Worry and fear can't come near me. For example, in Isaiah 54:4-17 we anchor our spirit in powerful words, ending with "No weapon formed against me will prosper." When any word is spoken against us that's not in or of the Word of God, we have the power and anointing as a child of God to rip those words out of the soil so they don't take root, and to replace them with the Word of God. In other words, we can practice truth versus lies as a lifestyle. Anytime we start feeling fear, we can ask, "What lie am I believing?" The Holy Spirit will tell us the lie we are believing. Next, all we need to do is ask, "What's the truth?" He will tell us the truth, the truth in the Scripture, the Way, the Truth, and the Life!

We cannot separate the Word from the Spirit. Some leaders and churches have tried to, but we cannot, because they are one and the same! We can live being continually filled with the Spirit, which is the Word. Ephesians 5:18 reminds us, "Keep on being filled with the Spirit". John 6:63 and 2 Timothy 3:16 add, "My Word is spirit." So. if we keep on being filled with the Word, we're being filled continually with the Spirit. If we are being continually filled with the Spirit, the Kingdom of God is ever expanding in us. This parallels Isaiah 9, "There is no end to the expansion of the Kingdom of God." When we keep declaring God's Word, the Kingdom will be exploding in us as a lifestyle. Then, there will be no place for the devil to sneak into cracks or crevices because we're expanding the Kingdom by expanding the Word which is the Spirit.

I'm free and worry free. I will live and not die. Whatever I do will prosper. As Joshua 1:8 declares that all we need to do is keep the word in our mouth, keep saying it and doing what it says. Then everything we do will prosper. But some people still say, "It does not prosper now. Not in me." They have no idea. Most people's setbacks and delays are the root-building season for the next great harvest. Please hear me again. Many people think "I'm not going to make it", when by the Spirit their setbacks and delays are growing real and deeper roots. Then, when the Spirit provides the next wave of victory by faith, that breakthrough is many times stronger and larger than our best effort before the setback came. When we face headwinds and troubled waters, we must keep declaring the Word aloud so that seeds of faith in our heart grow deeper roots to withstand the next storm.

Many of us, even in dynamic congregations, are prone to base our faith on what we sense (see, hear, touch, taste, smell) or on what we feel (emotions in our soul). The root system of God's Kingdom has nothing to do with how we feel. It has everything to do with truth. The LORD and His Word are absolute truth; they can't lie. What He started, He will finish. Philippians 1:6 and Matthew 28:18 promise that He's never going to leave us. He is going to finish everything He started. Nothing can stop Him. He delivers us from evil and from the evil one (Galatians 1:4). Not only does He save us and forgive us, but He also cleanses, purifies, fills, and delivers us in real time from this present evil age. While we live in this world system, we are not part of it, because greater is He who is in us than he who is in the world. In Him, we can walk into the gates of Hell and release the glory of heaven! We have been delivered from this present evil age. We actually believe this good news!

The Psalmist in 91:10 challenges us to dwell in the shelter the Most High God and do what He says. Then, no evil, no pain, no sickness, no pestilence can come near us. How about that reality? Also, in Psalm 103:20 we learn to speak God's Word, to give voice to His Word in order to release angels to perform God's Word. If we're continually declaring God's Word, He will provide tens of thousands of angels to make sure God's Word is performed for us because we inherit salvation.

Also, according to Luke 12:8, Hebrews 1:14, and Psalm 103:20, through our declaration of the Word, God plants His seeds of truth in our heart to grow a harvest of God's Kingdom in our life. By our declaration of faith in the Word, God also unleashes myriads of angels to perform God's Word on our behalf. Amen?

According to Mark 13, heaven and earth will pass away, but His Word will never pass away. So, if we continue in His Him, His Word in us will never pass away, and we inherit eternal life. We will never experience eternal death if we fully continue in the Word and Spirit. Our whole life becomes a living epistle full of promises. Every one of these verses is worth a sermon!

In 2 Corinthians 3, we discover that if we live the Word like Joshua day and night, day and night, day and night, then our whole life becomes a Word explosion. The Word of God in us dispels evil, sickness, disease, depression, darkness, depravity, and wickedness. None of them stand a chance against the One who is greater. And "in the way of righteousness there is life. In His pathway, there is no death" (Proverbs 12:28). Everything is established on the testimony of two or three witnesses, and both Bible covenants agree. Both the Hebrew Covenant and the New Covenant are true; one always confirms the other.

Jesus the Messiah teaches in Luke 6:38, "Give and it will be given, pressed down, shaken together, running over, and others will give into your life." We are blessed because we give.
Why would we not want to be blessed? Well, then, let's be a blessing by giving. Let's sow seeds! The best time to sow seeds is when we don't think we can. I can give you multiple examples, even from the Hebrew covenant, where patriarchs would sow in a time of famine and receive a 100-fold return. God's Word is true; He cannot lie!

We should not wait until a financial planner says it's a good time. We give even during the worst of times. We plant vineyards when in exile. We build houses when we have no hope. We practice the Word despite circumstances and watch God's Word produce!

Deuteronomy 8:18 teaches that God gives us the power to get well. Why? So we could have our own empire? No. But so He can establish His covenant on the earth. Proverbs 1:22 instructs us to be doers of the Word, and not just hearers. Be doers of the Word. What does that mean? Practice and do the Word. How can we put something into practice without saying it? We should not tell somebody who is in need, "Bless you. I hope you do well." Instead, we should give them what they need, then say, "Bless you. I hope you do well."

We have been practicing. Occasionally, we take our team to Chipotle where we will sit and wait for the Spirit's guidance. Then, when the Lord impresses us, we'll choose six or eight people in line. We buy all their food and then pray over them. Every time, our giving them physical food opens their hearts to spiritual food. Shall we practice similar giving in Jesus' name? Let's do the Word so we don't become deceived. Amen?

# NOW FAITH!

We will become a lot less picky or critical about how leaders craft their sermons when we pursue a lifestyle of practicing the Word ourselves (James 1:22). Ephesians 6:10 trains us to put on the full armor of God, including the shield of faith that extinguishes the flaming arrows of the evil one. What does the shield of faith look like in real life? Paul wrote this from a Roman prison cell while looking at Roman soldiers who wore custom fit armor. Their shields were the size of a medium-sized door, which would only protect them from arrows sent by the enemy from one direction. But in real life, our enemies are on all sides. We're surrounded by foes who are sly and strategic. If they can't get us from one way, they will open fire from another way.

However, the biblical shield of faith is not like a rectangle. The more appropriate design is like a bubble, totally encapsulating us from any direction, anywhere, and anytime. If we're sleeping, if we're rising, if we're working, or if we're praying, it doesn't matter. If we're in faith, which comes by hearing the Word of God, we're covered by immersion in His glory. That's the Psalms 91 reality. That's the shield of faith. Amen?

Galatians 3:13 promises we are redeemed from the curse of the law. Jesus became the curse so we could become the blessed, which means I am healed and prosper spiritually. I am healed and prosper mentally and emotionally. I am healed and prosper financially. Past threats of terror are part of the curse. Now, Jesus reversed all of that by grace through faith.

So, by trusting Jesus' Word in Mark 11:23, we can say to mountains of any kind, "Be moved. If we don't doubt, but believe that what we say is true, then they must obey us. According to 2 Peter 1:3, we have been given everything we will ever need for life and godliness. That includes the promise that we have the same power that raised Jesus from the dead (Ephesians 1:19), waiting for our words to release

His power. Can any mountain we face stand against the power that raised Jesus from the dead? No. Because God gives us everything we will ever need for life and godliness. Let's declare faith in Him from our spirit and release His power through our words. That's how we practice faith and how faith rises and grows!

The words that teach "Every cell in my body obeys the Word of God" comes from many clear Scriptures. We're not going quote them all. Most of them are from Paul who says that the life of Christ within us makes everything in our body cry out for His life to control and empower every cell. One of those verses is Romans 8:11, "The same spirit that raised Jesus from the dead will also quicken our fleshly mortal bodies."

I am not proposing that we can command every cell in our body to stand up to attention, then start worshipping and praising during the pain instead of moaning and complaining in the pain. But we do have a choice by the power of the Holy Spirit in our spirit to command our soul and our body to rise up in worship instead of to bow down in dismay. Our body is healed by God's Word In the name of Jesus, because according to James 4:7, we submit to God and resist the devil as a lifestyle. We should never stop submitting to God and we should never stop resisting the devil. We need to submit to God and resist the devil continually. We must do both. Amen?

So, I declare by faith in the Word: poverty, sickness, and death, get out. I have life, health, and wealth, because Jesus took the curse so I could receive His blessing. I know God's voice because I'm one of His sheep and his sheep hear and know His voice (John 10:27). I also confirm that I know all things, because 1 John 2:20 proclaims, "I have an anointing and I know all things." And that is because 1 Corinthians 2:16 says, "I have the mind of Christ inside of me." And Christ knows all things!

# NOW FAITH!

All of this truth is in His book. I have received wisdom and revelation (Ephesians 1:17, Colossians 1:9, and others). One goal of Bible Letters is that we would grasp by wisdom, revelation, and knowledge everything that is already ours in Christ Jesus. Amen? So, I am delivered because I know the truth (John 8:31-32). And the truth I know sets me free. Also, I am delivered because "greater is He who is in me than he who is in the world" (1 John 4:4).

Now, the joy of the Lord is my strength (Nehemiah 8:10), even when the wall is merely halfway down and when enemies are mocking us. Even then, joy can increase because joy is not an emotion. Joy is a reality in the glory of God who cannot fail. Add Philippians 4:4-7, "Don't worry about anything, but in everything with thanksgiving, let your prayers and petitions be known to God. And the peace of God, which passes all understanding, will guard your hearts and minds in Christ Jesus."

The next time our kids are in trouble or the next time someone says we're going to lose our job or the next time someone walks out of our church, we need not worry about anything. Oh, how I long that the Church would receive, believe, and practice these principles, these laws of faith! When it looks like all is hopeless, we must start with thanking the Lord. That is when God picks up His scepter of authority and crushes satan. We must start with thanksgiving. Giving thanks.

I am born again (John 3:3). I'm a brand-new species (2 Corinthians 5:17). The world system knows only a percentage of the population like me. Because God and I are one: a brand-new species. 1 Corinthians 6:17 declares that I speak the truth in love. Ephesians 4:4 affirms that I am growing into the full measure and maturity of Christ Jesus. I am committed to be just as He is in this lifetime (Ephesians 4:13-17). And 1 John 4:17 validates that I am going to proclaim the message of the Kingdom that I learned in secret.

These signs will follow me because I believe. I speak like Jesus because I have a new tongue. I command demons to leave, and they run away in fear. I lay hands on the sick and they get better. How and why? Because God's Word says so and I believe Him and His Word (Mark 16:14-20. I have authority. In Christ alone, I have all authority because Jesus won it back, He lives in me, and He shares His authority with me. I am going to walk in authority.

So, I am going to practice His Word, to apply the blood of Jesus over everything God has given me to influence this world. And everywhere I place my feet, the kingdom of God is going with me (Joshua 1:3). Satan will learn every time he touches me, he's going to pay seven times because the LORD is a God of seven-times-justice. Soon, the evil one is going to learn he's barking up the wrong tree, because he found a believer who really believes. According to John 11:40, Jesus asked, "Didn't I tell you that if you believe, you will see the glory of God?"

John 11:40 and Colossians 1:27 agree, "Christ is in you, the hope of glory." I will live and never experience death (John 7:51), because eternal life is to know him (John 17:3). For eternity, this Word that we confess with our mouth and believe in our heart will be the reality to know Him more, and more, and more, and more for trillions, and trillions, and trillions of years.

Friends in faith, this is the culmination of our chapters on living the faith. I hope it's been a blessing! I pray we never return to living by feelings. I hope we threw the spaghetti string enough ways that one of them stuck. Now we know that no one else is going to do this for us. We must practice our own planting, our own confessing, our own declaring, our own believing. Paul disciples Timothy in 1 Timothy 6:12 to "Fight the good fight of faith." Amen?

## NOW FAITH!

As we close, I will declare a prayer of faith, especially for anyone who needs spiritual, emotional, or mental healing, that you will be able to receive and believe. I am going to release God's Word, just as in Psalm 107:20, the LORD sends His Word to His people. He has called all of us sons and daughters to prophesy, to declare His Word with His authority in us.

So, in the name of Jesus Christ and by the authority of the Holy Spirit in me, I send His Word to friends from Northwest Canada to Florida, from Central America to New England, from Europe to Asia, from South America to Africa, and from the islands of the seas to every remote village around the world. I send His Word and release healing in spirit, soul, and body: faith, hope, love, peace, freedom, and deliverance. Every demon, you have to leave; you cannot stay. I speak peace. I speak health. I speak blessing. I declare for every brother and sister authentic commitment to practice Your Word. Lord, grant courage to each. Fulfill whatever your Word says, so each of us can do what Your Word says. I pray this in the name of Jesus Christ, Son of God, and Savior. Amen!

## ABOUT THE DAN BOHI

**DAN BOHI** is the founder of Becoming Love Ministries Association (formerly Dan Bohi Ministries Association) and his mission is to awaken the church of Jesus Christ to the power, purity, and freedom of the Spirit-filled life, found, realized, experienced, and exhibited in the live of believers in the Book of Acts! Dan has traveled the country for 15 years imparting the message of Holiness to pastors, leaders, and churches in over 25 denominations.

Since 2008, Dan continues to pursue the Lord's call as an itinerant minister. God's call on his life is to awaken the Church of Jesus Christ to the power, purity, and freedom of the Spirit-filled life, found, realized, experienced, and exhibited in the lives of believers in the Book of Acts. He and his wife Debbie enjoy four married children and fourteen grandchildren.

Dan has traversed the country from coast to coast, globally, and across many denominations, while retaining his basic biblical convictions. His ministry blends the Word of God and the power of the Holy Spirit. During his ministry in revivals, conferences, and other awakenings, pastors and other leaders confirm that thousands of participants experience encounters with the Lord. Entire congregations are impacted by Jesus and the Gospel.

Focused on spiritual transformation, he witnesses thousands of persons who come to faith in Jesus Christ. Thousands also receive baptism in the Holy Spirit, evidenced by cleansed, purified, empowered hearts and lives, producing fruit of the Holy Spirit. He watches the Lord fulfill His power in healing, freedom, deliverance, miracles, signs, and wonders, all predicated on authentic love in Christ.

Dan teaches and practices love. He believes that sincere believers pursue love first and always, avoid supernatural activity devoid of love, and desire only biblical, supernatural, Book-of-Acts ministries motivated with love by the indwelling Holy Spirit. He shares widely His testimony of God's grace and power as summarized here.

I was involved in a vehicle accident on the morning of June 15, 1995. I was hit by a crane truck and expended weeks in a Kansas hospital. My injuries were a broken pelvis, broken vertebrae, a lacerated liver, a torn urethra, many cuts and bruises, and my abdomen was full of blood.

All day during tests at the hospital, I kept having out of body experiences with an angel who kept me alive. I suspect he was there because my mom prays with faith and has influence with the Lord. When the day finally started winding down, I was placed in an ICU room. I did not know whether I would survive and wondered whether I could thrive.

That evening at 5:37 was the greatest moment of my life. I am forever changed because of what Jesus did for and in me that day. All those years He was patiently waiting for me. That evening was a celebration of Christ's victory in my life. He accomplished what I needed then and continues to provide what I need daily.

I was 34 years old and had tried for years to be free from fear, pride, lust, jealousy, depression, and anxiety. I tried hard but could never do

## NOW FAITH!

enough to experience lasting change in my life. That evening when I was at my weakest and lowest moment, Jesus came to me and spoke to my heart words that transformed my life for eternity.

The Lord assured me He had forgiven my sins. Then, He wanted to know when I would completely cease selfish control and give Him my life. I had been trying to do this for years in my own strength. In that moment, I simply trusted Him and said, "Yes, Lord, I am Yours completely."

In that moment the Lord accomplished supernatural cleansing in me, and I have never been the same since. He removed all the darkness in me and filled me with His glorious presence. My first witness of change: I felt no fear for the first time in my life.

Over the years since then I have always been aware that was the moment my heart was forgiven and set free, purified by the blood of Jesus Christ. I was filled with and baptized in the Holy Spirit. My desires and passions changed forever. I'm more in love with Him now than ever before. In fact, my love and hunger for Him grows daily.

My primary goal is to become a man who prays to the FATHER in the name of JESUS in the power of the SPIRIT according to the WORD. I do not want to do this merely in ministry preparation, or in public, or whenever trouble or pressure comes. I commit to pray this way without ceasing.

I commit to live in unbroken fellowship with my Father. I want to know Christ day by day, like never before. I want to know the voice of the Holy Spirit better. I want to become a man of patience and calm, full of wisdom and strength, meek and compassionate, slow to speak and quick to love. This is my desire: becoming love.

# DAN BOHI

## CONTACT:

If you would like to contact Dan for
a speaking event please visit:
**www.becomingloveministries.com**
or contact
Rev. Jim Williams at:
**jimwilliams@becomingloveministris.com**

Becoming Love Ministries
7905 NW 49th Street
Bethany, Ok 73008

---

www.ingramcontent.com/pod-product-compliance
Lightning Source LLC
Chambersburg PA
CBHW051044160426
43193CB00010B/1063